ERNIE ELS'
Guide to
Golf Fitness

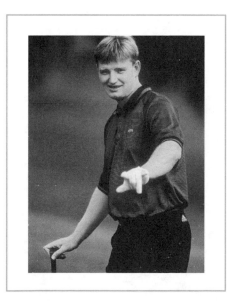

ERNIE ELS' Guide to Golf Fitness

How Staying in Shape
Will Take Strokes Off Your Game
and Add Yards to Your Drives

ERNIE ELS and DAVID HERMAN

Crown Publishers   NEW YORK

Also by ERNIE ELS

How to Build a Classic Golf Swing

The Complete Short Game

AUTHOR'S NOTE: This book proposes a program of physical exercise for the reader to follow. However, before starting this or any other exercise or fitness program, you should consult your physician.

Copyright © 2000 by Ernie Els and David Herman

Published by Crown Publishers, New York, New York.
Member of the Crown Publishing Group.

Random House, Inc. New York, Toronto, London, Sydney, Auckland
www.randomhouse.com

CROWN is a trademark and the Crown colophon is a registered trademark of Random House, Inc.

Printed in the United States of America

DESIGN BY LYNNE AMFT

Library of Congress Cataloging-in-Publication Data
Els, Ernie.
[Guide to golf fitness]
Ernie Els' guide to golf fitness : how staying in shape will take strokes off your game
and add years to your drives / Ernie Els and David Herman—1st ed.
1. Golf—Training. 2. Physical fitness. I. Title: Guide to golf fitness.
II. Herman, David, 1967– III. Title.
GV979.T68 E57 2000
613.7'11—dc21 99–047129

ISBN 0-609-60543-7

10 9 8 7 6 5 4 3 2 1

First Edition

Contents

Acknowledgments

WE'D LIKE TO THANK Nick Frangos, Jackie Point, Steve Szurlej, and Sheila Wallace for their assistance, support, and professional guidance.

A very special thanks to Crown Publishers and especially Peter Fornatale for his advice, assistance, and patience in completing this manuscript. Thanks also to Lynne Amft, Liana Faughnan, and Jean Lynch.

We are grateful for the support, help, and advice of the professionals and scientists who read and commented on this book: Larry J. Kolb, Eric Greeno, Richard Sokolowski, and Dr. Brian Wallace.

We would also like to thank Robert Baker, Fred Dolan, David Leadbetter, and Karen Palacios for their insights into golf fitness.

Also, David Lihn, John J. Kerr, Richard Marek, and Clyde Taylor deserve thanks for helping to make this book happen.

Frank Nobilo, whose words of wisdom are always welcome and appreciated, you are truly "the consultant."

Thanks to all of our friends at Adidas golf.

And William C. Lufler, Tommy Thompson, and the late Harry Hopman, for all your help.

Preface

THE GAME OF GOLF IS CHANGING. Today more players are heading to the fitness center than to the clubhouse bar. Sure, there will always be the out-of-shape player who knocks the ball a mile down the fairway, but right beside him will be many more healthy, fit players matching that distance because of their athleticism and conditioning. The *professional* golfer has also become a true athlete and big-time businessman. And working out has become an integral part of many players' routines. Why has the desire to be fit become so important to amateur and professional golfers alike?

Because these people understand the value of keeping fit and healthy. The physical and business dynamics of the sport have changed. Many touring professionals are evolving from being "golfers" to being conditioned athletes. Professional golfers are becoming full-time athletes and part-time businessmen. They manage many of the rigorous demands that full-time corporate executives and part-time amateur golfers have experienced throughout their working lives. They recognize that the unrelenting pressures of long, unpredictable hours require the stamina and alert mental outlook that being in shape provides.

Professional golfers deal with the stressful Fridays striving to make the cut and the anxious Sundays trying to earn the prize money. And don't forget the daily telephone calls across countless time zones in an attempt to manage the assorted demands of their professional endorsements, business commitments, and family responsibilities. The golfer who uses this stress to fuel his workout is far better off than the one who allows this pressure to eat at him. More important, professional golfers have come to comprehend the relationship between fitness and their worst career nemesis: *injury*. They desperately need to avoid it. And they prevent it by becoming physically and mentally fit—and staying that way. The basic benefits of working out include:
- better and more consistent performance
- staying injury free

- having a stronger mental focus
- gaining greater confidence

Se Ri Pak sat in my office in early October 1998 following her four LPGA Tour victories that year, including two majors. It was my first opportunity since the spring to ask her if she felt that all the physical training she had done with me had helped her game. We had spent up to three hours daily for a solid year getting her physically prepared for her rookie season. She said, "All the hard work we did definitely made my mind and body stronger. I used to think I wasn't strong enough, but all the weights, walking, running, and stretching made a big difference for me." Hard work made her confident that her body was prepared and could perform on demand.

When Frank Nobilo first brought Ernie Els into the gym, I asked him which exercises he liked and which ones he disliked. I explained my approach, which emphasizes cardiovascular training, strength (resistance) training, and flexibility, and told him that I wanted him to start slowly with progressive fitness training. For a golfer, it's important to have a fitness program that emphasizes gradual change. No one's going to swing a golf club well if they're too sore from heavy lifting. My goal for that first day was to make it *fun* for him—not to make him sore—and to challenge him enough to entice him to come back.

I needed to make sure that I established a connection with Ernie, understood his needs, and measured his enthusiasm. To motivate and stimulate him, I felt it was essential to understand what he really wanted, what would drive his commitment. Without commitment, the fitness program would never succeed. So we personalized his program and kept it interesting and challenging. Ernie incorporated it all into his lifestyle with well-deserved results.

How

I concentrate on trying to feel where the athletes are emotionally, mentally, and physically each day. I evaluate their mood to determine the workout for the day. If they have been sick or in any way incapacitated, I back off. If they are just feeling lazy or sorry for themselves, then I am going to push them. With Ernie, as well as with all the athletes I train, I made him see that, as good as he was, he could become even better by being fit.

There's no doubt that being in poor condition causes early fatigue. And that tiredness is an open invitation to skill loss and inevitable errors. Those who are physically fit know their bodies will be there for them when it counts. Conditioning will not only reduce the effects of physical fatigue, but help sustain longer periods of concentration. This will allow the athlete to maintain his or her skill level and stay focused throughout practice and competitive situations.

Had I Known Then What Pros Know Now . . .

As a nationally ranked athlete in top-five NCAA Division I Tennis competition, I was always getting hurt. It was as if my body wasn't made for sport. An injury here meant lost practice time. An injury there meant a missed tournament. Finally, at an NCAA tournament during my junior year, I had a career-ending injury followed by three surgeries. At that point I knew I wasn't heading for the professional tour. But I was determined not to let go of my passion for sports. If I couldn't make it to the top, I could certainly help others get there.

Because of my injuries and frustrating setbacks, I developed an abiding interest in the workings of the body and received a degree in exercise science from the University of South Carolina. I had begun to focus on the effects of conditioning on the athlete. I became intrigued with the obvious correlation between fitness and performance. As I strove to maximize my performance and overcome my physical limitations, I realized that physical training and conditioning were a necessity not only for the body, to enhance performance, but also for the mind and spirit, to gain the mental strength to control stress and anxiety.

Getting *You* from There to Here . . .

What about that gym membership you bought the family for Christmas, or that state-of-the-art home gym you bought in ten easy payments? What about the bike in the garage with the flat, or the in-line skates still in their box? Great intentions are frequently ambushed by unforeseen circumstances. The first step is to personalize the right exercise regimen to make it a pleasurable experience for you. The routine should make you want to come back for more.

Each of us has physical weaknesses. I want to help you to identify yours. Maybe you're overweight. Or maybe you are as tight as a two-by-four. Or maybe you are supple but lack strength. Let's focus on getting you connected with your body. That's my approach. It's like I told Ernie on the first day: For a while, you're going to be into a rhythm of working out regularly, and then you're going to drift out of it. Lapses in your program are inevitable. But the challenge is motivating yourself to get back into the routine. In this book, Ernie and I want to teach you how to listen to and, more important, feel your body—to tailor your physical fitness program to your lifestyle.

You can get involved in many ways: working out with your children at home, jogging with your spouse or friends, joining a health club, creating a mini-gym in your home. There are countless alternatives. The keys are convenience, enjoyment, and commitment. We'll help you find the best way to exercise.

My training techniques and programs are the result of ten years of observing, competing with, and training corporate and professional athletes. Conditioning is no longer a one-dimensional program of weight lifting and jogging. It is a combination of flexibility, strength, and cardiovascular endurance that will train the body to be a better athlete. My number one goal is to get you enthusiastic and excited about your own fitness. My second goal is to seek the level of conditioning you want (and need) and to customize a fitness program that fits your lifestyle. Whether you are a corporate or professional athlete, the more you understand *your* body and the type of conditioning *you* need—physical, mental, and emotional—the better an athlete and more successful a performer you will become.

DAVID HERMAN

ERNIE ELS'
Guide to
Golf Fitness

Introduction

I GREW UP IN SOUTH AFRICA playing a lot of sports—rugby, cricket, tennis, and golf. Since I was young and big and active, I never had to really worry about "working out." I just exercised naturally every day when I played. I never really thought about it. The sports themselves were my exercise.

My first experience with intense physical training was in the South African Air Force when I did my mandatory two years of service. It was here that I learned to hate exercise. I went into the military and they chased me around so much during the first six months that I vowed never to run again. My sergeant major must have been a frustrated track coach. I ran everywhere: to training, from training, to the mess hall, back to the barracks, to the bathroom. The only place I couldn't run was for cover. No one without four legs should ever have to run that much. I just said, *Enough*.

So I was determined to play golf professionally and not worry about being in great condition. I was young enough and stupid enough then to think that I would never get out of shape and, anyway, playing golf wasn't all that physically demanding. I was lazy. Golf was fun. I loved spending hours and hours on the course and the range, experimenting, playing, and refining my game—but that was play, not work.

A few years went by and I was doing very well. I was on the tour, never in great shape, but winning. Then in 1992, I won a string of South African PGA events, including the South African Open—as a matter of fact, six out of eleven tournaments—and finished fifth in the British Open. I won enough money to qualify for the European Tour without going to the Tour Qualifying School. What a year—and I hadn't done one push-up! I felt great: I developed my technique through countless hours of practice (I never considered this work), I was winning, I was thoroughly enjoying myself, I wasn't exercising (that *was* work), and I never thought about the sergeant major.

Then in 1994 I won the U.S. Open at the Oakmont Country Club in western Pennsylvania. I was twenty-four years old, feeling very confident (maybe a little bit cocky), and delighted to be considered a world-class player. But I knew for the first time everything wasn't quite right: I had been exhausted after that Open week.

I had arrived at Oakmont early, on Monday, raring to go (I had finished second in the Buick Classic the week before) and played 18 practice holes on Monday, Tuesday, and Wednesday—54 holes total. It was really hot. Thursday and Friday I played well. But the temperature was awful: over one hundred degrees and muggy. On Thursday, several golfers melted down and withdrew—a few by ambulance. On Sunday I began to feel the heat and finally experienced its effects on the crucial eighteenth hole. I needed a par to win. I teed off and pulled my shot way to the left, into the trees. Nerves weren't the crucial factor. It was fatigue creeping in. I salvaged a bogey.

My reward was 18 more holes the next day in a three-man play-off with Loren Roberts and Colin Montgomerie. Through even more heat Loren and I struggled to a two-man tie. On the second sudden-death hole Loren made a mistake and bogeyed. I made par and won. That was *92* tournament holes in *five* straight days, in stifling heat, preceded by those 54 practice holes. Eight days in a row, 146 holes of pressure golf in strenuous and challenging conditions. I survived more on my will to win than on the condition of my body. The next afternoon I lay down and just passed out. That week I flew to England, totally exhausted, mentally and physically, and wound down.

I was beginning to think differently about the sergeant major.

I sensed it was time for a change in my life. But I downplayed my exhaustion and blamed it on the heat. After all, I was happy with one of my best years on the golf course: the U.S. Open, World Match Play, the Dubai Desert Classic, the South African Open, the Johnnie Walker World Championship, and the Gene Sarazen World Open wins. I was young, fearless, and playing on an adrenaline rush. I was just naturally in good shape.

In 1995, I finished third in the PGA Championship after carrying a three-shot lead into the final. At the British Open I shot a seventy-five in the last round and lost by four strokes. I had some bad rounds at the end of the year. I was tired at the wrong time. I didn't want to believe it, but I sensed a pattern beginning to develop.

So I decided to get fit, hoping for fast results. I worked with a fitness trainer, but a week of intense exposure to heavy weights and exercise bicycles created too much sudden strain and too many aches. It was a shock to my system, not a gradual benefit. My trainer had good intentions, but as a golfer, and physically unfit, I realized that this quick cure was not the right approach. I was so sore I couldn't move. This sudden activity clearly was not what my body needed. Waterskiing was better exercise.

But I did realize that I needed conditioning. The game was getting more competitive, and the good golfers—the ones who were winning—were in shape. And there was Gary Player, my idol, at sixty-two still looking great and playing and winning. *He* was in shape!

My winning continued. But in 1996, I lost the British Open and came in second with, again, last-round problems: bogeys on sixteen and eighteen. In 1997 I won the U.S. Open again. The next week I won the Buick Classic. But as the April-to-August season wore on, so did I. I finished tenth in the British Open, and in the Buick Open in Detroit shot seventy-four in the final round and blew a lead. It seemed that every year from 1994 to 1997, I was wearing out as the season went on. I was dead tired by August. My best finish in the PGA Championships during those four years was third, but in the other three years I never finished better than the top forty-five.

In August 1997, while still celebrating my second U.S. Open title, I saw myself on the cover of *Golf World* magazine. They had taken a picture of me lying on a raft in a pool, with a beer in my hand and excess flab around my waist. I saw that and said, *Ouch!* I was embarrassed—my body had to change. It was time to burn some fat, and I needed a new approach.

But I still resisted the hard work. Then my good mate Frank Nobilo started to needle me about my flabby cover shot. He had been working out with a physical conditioning coach who had a reputation for developing specific exercise programs for us golfers. I am 6'3" and know I don't have to pump weights like Gary Player, who is 5'8", or run wind sprints all day like my sergeant major.

I had heard about Dave Herman from Frank and from my swing coach, Robert Baker, who told me that Dave had a distinct approach with his golfers. The word was that he carefully analyzed each athlete, assessed their needs, and slowly developed and customized a fitness program for them.

So despite bad memories of running and my recent bad experience with a trainer, I decided it was time to finally step up and quit kidding myself. I had to get into shape. The game itself had changed—it was a more athletic sport than it had been.

Frank, who was older and had been through a few injuries, reminded me that sooner or later my body would catch up with me—and that it's much easier to prevent an injury than it is to heal one. With his years of experience on the tour, the Kiwi was looking after me. He realized how much I traveled. I was one of the few golfers who played all over the world. With thirty to thirty-four tournaments a year—and flying out of South Africa to the United States for half of them—jet lag, travel fatigue, and cramped muscles start to take a lot out of your body.

Dave understood that I didn't have to (and I didn't want to) be a Mr. Universe to be a fit golfer. He designed a program that got my heart pumping (without running!), my muscles toned, and kept my body stretched and limber.

We started slowly and took it easy. With stretching and toning and cautious training, we have developed a program that fits my needs. My swing now has more speed. My shot-making is a lot more consistent. I have more power and flexibility—I feel looser and stronger.

And, just as important, my fitness program has strengthened my mind. Working out can pick up your moods and really help turn a bad day into a good one.

I saw Dave's program work. I am physically and mentally tougher. My energy level is high. I always feel I can bounce back after weeks off at a time. I have more strength and endurance; I feel more relaxed and in command. And the bonus? I burned off fifteen pounds and feel like an athlete again.

Now you—the corporate athlete with the same traveling, scheduling, and pressure demands—have to resolve to get your body and mind fit. Start slowly. Work through these chapters, follow Dave's advice, and benefit from my experiences. Adapt to your body and push yourself to what you want to be. Work on your flexibility, get your heart rate up, cut out the cholesterol. There are no gimmicks or shortcuts. It's hard work, but it will also be fun and rewarding. And you can do it your way and see your body and game change—get them back to what you want them to be.

You'll look better and feel better and score better.

Join me in being fit for golf and fit for life.

ERNIE ELS

CHAPTER ONE

The Corporate Golfer

*Fun and stress, challenge and anxiety, failure and success—the pro golfer and the
executive are two clubs in the same golf bag. We compete, we keep score, we take
risks, we get stuck in a trap, we scramble back, we recover. But most of all, we play
to win. And* nothing *increases our chances of victory—on the eighteenth hole or in
the boardroom—like being in sound physical and mental condition.*

ERNIE ELS

Introduction

THE WORK ETHIC, LIFESTYLE, needs, and aspirations of the successful
touring golfer and the corporate golfer are remarkably similar. Both professionals work
hard, juggle countless demands, and balance conflicting schedules. Both must prepare,
study, and train constantly, as well as formulate strategies and battle stress. Both hate to
lose and love to compete and to win.

All businesspeople are loaded down with projects, deadlines, conferences, work,
and time conflicts. The touring pro is overwhelmed with media commitments, fan

demands, practice sessions, and competitive play. The pressures for both are often unrelenting and grinding.

And, most significant, there is no off-season in either work arena. Most sports players have a well-defined break with a period of active rest. Not the PGA Tour player, and certainly not the corporate executive.

My schedule usually consists of three or four tournaments in succession, followed by a week or two off. Depending on scheduling, tournament results, and other commitments, I might take several weeks off during the year. But "off" doesn't mean *off*. It means photo shoots, long hours of practice, and increased time in the gym. It means preparing myself for the important events. I want to be at the very top of my game for the majors. Ten days before each of the four tournaments I begin my intense preparations, building on my conditioning and fitness so I know I'll be at my best. Preparing my body and mind helps me deal with the pressure of competition. As a result of my increased stamina, strength, and flexibility and the confidence that comes with them, I perform better on the course.

And there is an added benefit to my fitness program. My workouts not only make me tougher in the face of stress, but the exercise actually *releases stress*. I am in my own space, forgetting the problems and concentrating on the effort. I feel inspired and invigorated.

The busy, overworked corporate executive will experience the same benefits by making a commitment to exercise. By getting yourself in better shape you'll be able to fight off fatigue more easily. You'll also have a better chance of avoiding injury. Another benefit is that your body will be resilient, enabling you to play three rounds of golf in a weekend— and *well*. And best of all, being in shape can mean longer drives that will put you in a better position to lower your score.

The Benefits of Conditioning

Professional golfers have never been billed as strong, rugged, fit, or muscled. Some are lean, some portly, some tall, many short, but golfers were never really accorded the athletic respect given to swimmers, marathoners, or tennis players. But golfers today are rapidly changing the perception.

A spring 1998 article in *Sports Illustrated* titled "A Shape of Things to Come" highlighted the changes:

The current crop of top Tour players, though, plus many older pros, are exploding those myths about golf and musculature while changing the shape of golfers, if not the game. The new breed has made working with weights as much a part of its daily routine as breaking out a new glove. . . . Underneath all those billowy shirts and pleats, the world of pro golf is becoming filled with flat-stomached, broad shouldered, finely tuned power-packs. . . .

And how does this "trend" stand up? Does getting stronger really benefit the body for golf? Does cardiovascular conditioning really help on the golf course? The answer is a resounding yes. (Check out the *Golf* magazine article from January 1999, "Fit to a Tee.")

Today, fitness, stretching, body toning, and weight training are as much a part of the tour as caddies, chip shots, and courtesy cars. . . . As the millennium approaches, golfers of all ages, shapes, and sizes realize that proper physical fitness translates to fiscal fitness, stamina, and longevity in a lifelong sport. *Exercise is in.*

Why is this so? Well, look at me. I shed fifteen pounds and gained the stamina I was lacking during the dog days of summer. Tom Lehman lost twenty-five pounds. Mark O'Meara had similar results: "The most noticeable difference has been how fresh I have felt during the last few holes of each round and how much energy I have had on Sundays."

A *New York Times* editorial page article from September 27, 1998, highlighted some interesting facts about exercise. It wasn't until the 1930s that people even accepted the idea that heavy exercise was good for you. Apparently, physicians concerned about the health and longevity of university oarsmen in England and the United States discovered "to their surprise that the oarsmen were living longer than the general population." And Finnish endurance athletes lived six years longer than their less active neighbors. Further, the article refers to a survey of fifty-two thousand men from two Ivy League universities conducted over a thirty-four-year period by a Stanford University medical professor. Dr. Ralph S. Paffenberger's study "shows that men who exercise hard and regularly tend to live longer." Expending two thousand calories a week in vigorous activities (the equivalent of jogging or briskly walking twenty miles) "brought a 25 percent reduction in the chance of dying during the study period." His rule of thumb is that for each hour of vigorous exercise "you get an extra two or three hours of life . . . but exercise affects more than just the quantity of life. It also improves its quality by making people feel healthier."

Phasing In—The Commitment Cycle

We all go through phases in our lives, and exercising is no exception. One week you're in an enthusiastic exercise mode, but before you know it, you drift out. It happens to all of us! Sometimes we just don't have control over when it's possible to exercise, and we often feel guilty for losing our exercise momentum. Days go by without exercising and before you know it you feel like you have lost your drive. The change in desire can occur so rapidly that you might not even feel it coming on.

What causes this lapse? It could be a flu bug that creeps up on you. It might be a vacation with the family. A four-day business trip can throw you out of sync. A PGA touring professional goes through periods of confidence and commitment when he plays and trains. An executive goes through periods of increased workloads and time conflicts.

Your fitness plan should be a twelve-month strategy, but calculated to give you a guilt-free week off here and there. Fit it into your lifestyle. We want to give you strategies on how to phase in after you have been out. I have found that after a layoff, it often takes five to ten days to get back and get connected. Dave will explore certain nutritional supplements that work well in boosting energy levels and might help you push through the struggle of phasing into your workouts (we will mention these supplements and their effects in chapter 9, "Nutrition"). Once you complete these first five or so workouts, you will begin to feel a renewed sense of motivation. It's important to remember not to overtrain in these first sessions back. Getting so sore that you need more days off isn't going to help you one bit.

We want your conditioning curve to be progressive. Start slowly and build gradually. Remember that if you stay with it, you'll look back and smile. We are not trying to get you in shape in four weeks. Look at this training as I do—as exercise for the long haul. We are trying to show you a way to change your approach to fitness by adding new ideas to your current program—to keep you motivated not just for now, but for life.

Commitment

Most of Dave's corporate clients want to do two things—lose weight and increase their flexibility. Burning body fat and lowering my cholesterol were initially my biggest concerns, and they are the most likely concerns of the corporate golfer. Once I met these goals I switched my focus to keeping injury free and maintaining my endurance.

Meeting your goals doesn't mean you have to kill yourself at the gym. In an interview in *Golf Digest* in August 1998, Lee Trevino talked about the weight loss that had sparked a reawakening on the course for him:

> Amazing, isn't it? I woke up last Christmas morning; I looked in the mirror and I almost ran out of glass. I was 206 pounds. Too much. By March, I was down to 190. And I'm aiming at 180.

His approach to exercise? Simple: "I'm doing the treadmill, maybe three miles at a crack. Nothing crazy." Even if you have only fifty minutes two times a week, you'll be able to see a real difference in your body and in your game.

The key to the success of any program is commitment. And commitment doesn't mean that you have to be obsessive about the gym. In fact, the best way to stay committed is to make sure that your program works for you. And remember that lapses are okay. Just make sure they don't become permanent. The goal is to enjoy the results of your workout.

CHAPTER TWO

Tailored to Your Needs

Don't jump into an exercise program because you suddenly think you want to get into shape and you can condition your body in a quick week, just like the old days. Consider what you want your body to accomplish and gradually—and intelligently—devise a fitness program that will get you there. I don't need big biceps and the chest of Hercules to play better golf, and my training reflects that. No pain, no gain? That's silly. Don't hurt yourself; train yourself. Give yourself time, make your workout fun, then count down the pounds and the handicap.

ERNIE ELS

Introduction

IT'S IMPORTANT TO CHOOSE an exercise program that you enjoy. If your workout fits your lifestyle, you will be motivated to do it consistently and efficiently—even on the days you don't feel energized. Your exercise routine should provide you with a comfortable, challenging routine that you can adjust according to your energy level.

Your exercise program should make you fit for golf. It can enhance your performance and lower your handicap. It will also give you a stronger body, a healthier frame of mind, more energy, and better concentration. You should tailor your fitness program to your physical needs and your individual goals.

Identify Your Body Type

Each of us must be aware of the characteristics and limitations of our bodies in order to analyze and identify our individual fitness needs. Dave has explained to me the various physical characteristics that make each of us different and unique.

How would you classify your physique? How do you describe your physical condition? In order to help you design your conditioning program, you must first distinguish your body type. Here are the three basic choices:

1. **Ectomorphs** are slim-muscled, thin-boned people who have little body fat and can struggle to gain muscle mass—golfers such as Tiger Woods, Justin Leonard, and Helen Alfredsson are representative of this group. Weight gain in these people usually develops in the stomach area. They tend to have a high metabolic rate and are generally good at endurance activities but may want to add strength and power to their game.

2. **Mesomorphs** are naturally thicker boned and have more muscle mass, bulk, and weight—Se Ri Pak and I are good examples. Mesomorphs are naturally stronger than ectomorphs and tend to be more powerful. Cardiovascular exercise is essential for mesomorphs because of their tendency to increase body fat when inactive. Mesomorphs also must be careful not to do too much heavy weight training, because they can bulk up easily.

3. **Endomorphs** tend to be heavy or overweight, soft, and low in muscle tone, with a tendency to gain weight. Endomorphs need to be cognizant of their eating habits, and workouts should be centered on light toning exercises with low-intensity fat-burning activities. Their primary exercise goal is to decrease their weight (and body fat percentage).

Adapt to Your Body

Many individuals don't fit perfectly into any of these three categories. But the classifications are important indicators of golf swing styles and physical fitness tendencies. The ectomorph, unless he or she has a flabby stomach, does not want to emphasize fat-burning activities, but wants to spend more time concentrating on increasing strength and maintaining flexibility. This means the ectomorph wants to spend more time in the weight room, probably doing fewer reps with slightly heavier weights than the average golfer.

The mesomorph, on the other hand, must be careful not to do too much lifting of heavy weights. Instead, he or she should focus on doing more reps with lighter weights. The mesomorph generally will also have to spend more time focusing on cardiovascular exercise than the ectomorph.

A typical endomorph is overweight and, if not active, has a tendency to put on weight very easily. An endomorph's program usually requires a great deal of low-intensity cardiovascular exercise. Endomorphs need to lose body fat to remove the extra stress on their joints before they begin high-impact cardiovascular workouts such as running. When it comes to weight training, the endomorph doesn't want to build muscle mass but needs to tone his or her muscles by doing high reps of lighter weights with short rest periods between exercises.

Be aware of your body. Define your deficiencies. Counter your negatives. Don't be judgmental. If you insist on smoking or eating too many doughnuts (despite the scientific evidence that smoking causes cancer and doughnuts make you fat), go ahead, do what makes you happy. But you must at least try to compensate for it by doing the physical exercise to counter the negative effects (and diminish the guilt). Aim for cardiovascular exercise. Run it off. Bike it off. Swim your guilt away.

Once you classify your body type and understand your strengths and weaknesses, establish the program that works for you.

Take the Next Step

When Frank Nobilo introduced Dave Herman to me, I weighed 230 pounds and had a high cholesterol count. I was fearful of getting involved in a structured exercise routine.

I had jumped into an intense exercise program for a week and became so muscle sore I now wanted to avoid working out.

Dave had started working with Frank in June 1997, and they had developed a solid working friendship. Often during their workouts Frank would speak to Dave about me and how I needed to get up off the couch and take care of my body. One day in October, Frank convinced me to accompany him to the gym. I was a little nervous; the memory of the muscle soreness was lingering. The next morning we both walked in. Frank was nice enough to work out by himself, allowing Dave to help me get a feel for what conditioning I needed to benefit my body and my golf game. Over the next two weeks, we worked out eight times.

For me, getting started on the right program was all it took. You've got to do the same. Start off by trying some of the sample workouts in chapter 8; feel free to adjust our sample programs to meet your own needs and interest. A few weeks after working out with Dave for the first time, I was already reaping the benefits. I won the Grand Slam of Golf tournament over Tiger Woods, Justin Leonard, and Davis Love III in Hawaii. I'm not going to tell you that my new workout program had everything to do with my victory, but I will tell you that I knew right away that working out was going to have positive effects on my game.

Fitness Analysis

When I began his program, Dave did for me what he does for every golfer. He analyzed and evaluated four major areas of my physical fitness—my flexibility, my strength and muscular endurance, my cardiovascular fitness, and my history of injuries. Through a series of tests, he measured: (1) the strength of my upper body (moderate chest presses and lat rows); (2) my legs (leg presses); and (3) my abdominal muscles (modified sit-ups).

Dave then measured my cardiovascular condition by monitoring my heart rate. He set a treadmill at 4 mph, on a 1 percent elevation, and had me walk for eight minutes. The treadmill indicated that my heart rate was in the 140-to-150 range. This was high. Clearly my program had to be designed to emphasize cardiovascular training (we chose the stair climber and stationary bike for this).

Next, Dave performed a series of specific flexibility tests on my hips, hamstrings, lower and upper back, and shoulders (incidentally, I learned that a right-handed player's left side—hips and lower back—is generally tighter).

As a result of the testing, we determined the following:

- My body fat percentage was too high (by 12 to 15 percent).
- My cardiovascular system was underperforming (after I hit the top of my target heart rate zone, it took me three minutes—it should have taken one—to recover).
- I had to strengthen my abdominal muscles and lower back to develop and maintain a strong trunk.
- Specific shoulder exercises were needed to prevent shoulder soreness from recurring rotator cuff strains.
- My exercises were designed to tone my upper body as well as strengthen my trunk and lower body.
- I needed to maintain my natural range of motion through flexibility and stretching exercises.

The program Dave created consisted of:

1. light strengthening exercises that focused on toning the upper body (not adding muscle mass and creating muscle soreness);

2. strengthening the legs (but not overdeveloping certain muscles that could decrease rotational speed);

3. strengthening and toning the "core" (the muscles of the center of the body—abdomen, obliques, hips, and lower back);

4. aerobic base training followed by high-intensity interval training (rigorous cardiovascular exercise—see chapter 4);

5. stretching to decrease muscle soreness and maintain and improve flexibility.

Most important, Dave emphasized proper posture to protect the spine during all exercises. He used the cardiovascular equipment (the stationary bike and the stair climber) to help develop strength and endurance in my legs. Interval training with these machines allowed us to create a strong resistance but not bring on any muscle soreness.

We used trunk stabilization exercises to develop the core muscles and dumbbells to train the upper body. The stretching exercises targeted my tight areas and focused on maintaining my flexible ones.

You may not be able to spend an hour with Dave. But if you use common sense and take into account your body type and your history of injuries, it's quite possible to devise your own workout plan by listening to your body. Of course, if you don't feel comfortable doing this, you can always contact a physical therapy group or a professional trainer who specializes in working with golfers, or with athletes in general.

Your Exercise Prescription

Improving your fitness could be the key element in breaking into a higher level of athletic performance. Recognizing and working to improve your body's physical limitations can help you improve motor skills, increase club head speed, and correct swing flaws.

We found the study that proves it. This one, of senior recreational golfers, reported by Wayne Westcott and John Parziali in the December 1997 issue of *Fitness Management,* demonstrated that combining strength training with stretching exercises produced a five-mile-per-hour increase in club head speed during an eight-week program. *We're talking about more yards on your driver.*

General lack of conditioning can certainly be a cause for decreased performance on the course. Most of us are aware that as we get older, we get weaker and tighter and our bodies don't seem to recover as quickly from physical exertion. We are stiffer in the morning, and we don't loosen up as quickly as we used to. Part of the problem is that as we get older we naturally lose lean muscle mass, increasing our percentage of body fat and becoming less flexible. Knowing this should be enough to motivate us to take action.

But what can be done about this? We're going to answer that question with a question: What form of exercise is it that you enjoy doing?

Again, we want your physical fitness program to be tailored to you. If you love running, then run. If you enjoy lifting weights, then work out with weights. If you enjoy stretching or taking a yoga class, then get to class! "Exercise" does not mean spending an hour in the gym six days a week. It is a battle cry to help you get started, to keep you challenged, to give you motivation and help you improve your golf game and overall feeling of well-being. First, you must become more aware of how important the condition of your body is to improving your swing and your health (and your outlook).

You don't need an expensive gym and state-of-the-art equipment to get or stay in shape. You can achieve a great workout without having to take the time to run to the local gym.

"TAILORED" EXERCISES

A friend of Dave's who lives in New York City has for the past fifteen years used Central Park and a tree branch as an integral part of his fitness center. During Dave's last visit they went to the park and went for a run. When they were finished, his friend trotted over to his favorite tree to do his pull-ups and some stretching, but the branch was gone. No worries, though—he quickly found another tree with a thick branch. The point is that once you're motivated, you can't let circumstances get in the way of your workout. Don't allow yourself to be discouraged, and feel free to be creative.

Robert Baker is my swing coach in Orlando, Florida. Robert has converted his garage into a training room. Autographed pictures from many of the game's greatest players hang on his walls. In the corner sit dozens of clubs. Along the wall are rows of dumbbells. Off to the side are a weight-lifting bench, a stretching apparatus, and a small area where Robert can swing clubs. If he added a cardiovascular machine, he would have a golf-specific fitness gym. But he chooses to do his cardiovascular training at the clubhouse pool.

While traveling on business or vacation, do what you have to do but try to give yourself half an hour to work out at the hotel gym or go for a run around the park.

In Conclusion

When it comes to exercise, you've got to do whatever is realistic and practical for you. But let me give you some ideas on how to keep your program simple, productive, and challenging:

- Do exercises you enjoy: cross-train by running, biking, swimming, cardioboxing, etc.
- Keep your workouts under one hour.
- Work out a minimum of two to three times per week.

- Concentrate on three areas of training:
    conditioning your lungs
    strengthening your muscles
    stretching your body
- Mix and combine all three areas at each session—pump, run, and stretch during your session.

Is it worth it?

Well, wait until it's all on the line as you're walking up to the green on eighteen after a long weekend of golf. You make the birdie putt to finish the round. At that moment, you know that you have just taken your game to a new level: one of fitness, stamina, concentration—and accomplishment. The fact is that win or lose, you want to know that you were at your best over each shot—that you gave yourself the best chance possible. Has all the dedicated work paid off?

Check your scorecard, your waistline, and your smile. You'll like what you see.

CHAPTER THREE

Warming Up

Prepare Your Body and Mind for the Front Nine

*You would never go into the boardroom for an important meeting
without collecting your thoughts and consulting your notes; you would never make
a presentation or speech without preparation and rehearsal. Why, then, would
you even consider teeing off without the proper warm-up? We are always
anxious and nervous at the first tee—we want to get on with it,
impress our mates. If your body is cold and your muscles are stiff,
your backswing will be a quick jerk and your swing awkward. There will be
no rhythm. Like any athlete, you need a warm-up routine.*

ERNIE ELS

The Basic Principles

WARMING UP AND STRETCHING will increase the ability of the
muscles to create more power and speed in your swing and prevent potential injuries.
The athleticism of golf requires synchronization of many moving parts. Don't

overlook or underestimate this truth. Warming up is *essential* to quality athletic performance.

Athletes of every sport prepare for their game with gradual, progressive loosening rituals. Whether it's a runner stretching before a race or a tennis player on the practice court, the athlete must prepare his body for competition. They all warm up their bodies and prepare their minds. When was the last time you played softball and didn't warm up your arm before you heaved a long throw from the outfield?

Golf, too, is a sport that requires careful physical and mental preparation. Warming up fires the engine of your body and allows you to rev up and perform. Warming up permits you to mentally focus and contemplate your game plan. It also lets you assess how your body feels and stretch out the areas of tightness and discomfort. This prevents potential injury and the frustration of a slow start and a clumsy shot by building rhythm and timing before you even get started.

I flew from South Africa to the Byron Nelson Classic in Dallas on a Sunday in 1998. I was not prepared for the jet lag that had crept up on me and was about to impact my performance. Without the proper warm-up (I did not have a warm-up ritual at that point), I was unaware of just how stiff and out of sync I really was. Dave said I looked sluggish, and I admitted to feeling a little groggy. On the first hole I mis-hit an approach shot and barely cleared the creek, leaving the ball forty yards short of the green. This set the tone for an exasperating day of golf.

During that day, I never achieved a flow nor created the physical and mental momentum necessary to play my best. By not appropriately warming up, I robbed myself of the opportunity to focus, build my confidence, and dominate the round early on. You can't expect to roll out of bed in the morning, compete well, and avoid injury without a good warm-up before your round.

Active Movement

The most effective way to begin your warm-up is to progressively simulate the movements of the activity you are about to pursue. In the process, you hope to gradually increase your body temperature.

Begin your warm-up by performing a series of golf-specific motions at a steady, slow pace. Experiment with the following series of five simple motion exercises that Dave taught me. Use them at the office, at home, in the clubhouse, or on the practice range.

We call this sequence of drills "the five-minute warm-up." It can be used effectively on its own or in addition to hitting a bucket of balls.

A reminder from Dave: Each of these exercises should be performed for about 1 minute. Obviously, you may repeat or extend the exercise if you feel the need for further limbering. Or you may devise your own regimen. The idea is to create motion and warm your body. Keep in mind that if any exercise tweaks an injury—even in this warm-up stage—it must be avoided. Listen to your body.

Wood Chop

Stand erect (concentrate on good posture), with your knees slightly bent, back straight, and feet slightly wider than shoulder width. Hold a telephone book, medicine ball, or similarly weighted object firmly above your head, with your arms fully stretched, and gently extend the object behind your head (Figure 1). Inhale and make a smooth downward wood-chopping motion with the object (Figure 2). Be careful that you do not jerk or bounce as the object flows through your legs (Figure 3). As you lift the object to the starting position, stretch back and exhale (Figure 1). Repeat this movement for 30 to 60 seconds.

Caution: Use a light weight (2 to 4 pounds), move slowly, and do not bounce.

FIGURE 1

FIGURE 2

FIGURE 3

Round the Clock

Stand erect (concentrate on good posture), with your knees slightly bent, back straight, and feet slightly wider than shoulder width. Hold a telephone book, medicine ball, or similarly weighted object firmly above your head, with your arms fully stretched (Figure 1). Slowly complete a circle moving the extended weighted object to your right (Figure 2), past your right knee to the floor (Figure 3), rotating your trunk, and returning to the standing, upright, fully extended position (Figure 1). Now repeat that circle, moving to your left (Figure 4). Continue for 1 or 2 minutes. Stretch through a full range of motion.

Caution: Make sure you keep your knees slightly bent and your back in a safe, neutral position. Use a light weight (1 to 4 pounds).

FIGURE 1

FIGURE 2

FIGURE 4

FIGURE 3

Lying Trunk Rotation

Lie flat on your back on the floor, arms stretched out to both sides. Bring your knees up until your feet are roughly 12 inches from the floor. Be sure to keep your lower back pressed to the floor (Figure 1). Slowly rotate your knees to one side, keeping your shoulder blades pressed to the floor (Figure 2). Stop at a comfortable stretch. Return to center and rotate your knees to the other side (Figure 3). Slowly work back and forth for approximately 1 minute. Try to keep an even flow of motion and stretch gently. Exhale as your legs lower to the floor and be careful not to push yourself past what is comfortable.

FIGURE 1

FIGURE 2

FIGURE 3

Standing Trunk Rotation

Stand erect, feet shoulder width apart and knees slightly bent. Place a golf club on your shoulders behind your neck and bend forward slightly, grasping the ends of the club with your hands. Rotate your upper body, creating the same movement that you would with your swing, bringing your front shoulder back toward the midpoint of your body (Figure 1). From the top of your backswing motion, rotate your body and complete the swing (Figure 2). Repeat this slow, controlled motion back and forth for 30 seconds, then add a second club and repeat for 30 seconds.

FIGURE 1   FIGURE 2

Two-Club Swing

Begin by taking your normal stance in an address position (Figure 1). Slowly swing a club back and forth in a smooth, rhythmic manner. Perform this for 30 seconds, then add a second club for an additional 30 seconds (Figure 2). Concentrate on staying relaxed throughout the exercise. Be sure to inhale on the backswing and exhale on the downswing and follow through (Figure 3).

Caution: If there is any pain, stop. **Listen to your body.**

FIGURE 1   FIGURE 2   FIGURE 3

The Stretch

Now that circulation is stimulated and muscle temperature is raised, you should stretch. Again, gradual motion is necessary. You are beginning to stretch muscles that inherently resist lengthening. The muscles are tight because of inactivity. Stretching not only increases muscle elasticity, but also will enable your muscles to contract more efficiently, creating more power in your swing.

As we demonstrate in chapter 6, stretching and flexibility could even be the focus of an entire workout. But do not diminish the importance of stretching during the crucial warm-up stage. Stretch before and after you work out. Many of the pros on tour stretch carefully and constantly. If you go right to the bar after a match, you get stiff. Do stretches after a hot shower. Or before you go for that beer, take five minutes and have a stretch. Four good warm-up stretches for golf are the Hamstring Stretch (page 103), the Lower Back Rotational Stretch (page 108), the Lat Stretch (page 101), and the Chest Stretch (page 100).

This is a very good rotational stretch to use that creates upper and lower back flexibility.

CHAPTER FOUR

Cardiovascular Conditioning

Tire and You Lose Your Fire

Whether you're running a business, running an errand, running for office, running to work, or running for cover, our bodies remind us that rapid movement—cardiovascular exercise—is part of our daily lives. At the conference table, in the home, on fields of play, we perform better if we are physically fit, mentally alert, and eager to achieve. That energy comes from feeling good and being in shape.

DAVID HERMAN

Introduction

ONE ESSENTIAL INGREDIENT of your physical fitness program—and Ernie is now a believer—is cardiorespiratory exercise. Strengthening your heart and lung capabilities is the key component to your conditioning regimen. Cardiovascular exercise, and the commitment it entails, is one of the best and most significant enhancements for your general health and well-being. Cardiovascular training will not only benefit your body by enhancing your stamina, energy, focus, and confidence, but also enable you to burn unwanted body fat at a highly efficient rate.

Certainly we know cardiovascular exercise is good for us. Countless magazine and newspaper articles tell us so. Television, cable, radio, the Internet, and videotapes feature exercise programs. Bookstores have entire sections devoted to physical fitness, and shelves full of books extolling the life-sustaining virtues of exercise. Library stacks are filled with medical journals stating the benefits of cardiovascular conditioning.

Getting Started

First, you have to take into consideration your current physical condition. Before beginning any exercise program it is strongly recommended that you visit your doctor for a medical examination. Review your past injuries. Consider your age and the amount of exercise you have been doing in the past year. Perhaps a stress test is appropriate, because it will allow you to know how your heart is working and alert you to any health problems of which you need to be aware.

You may test your level of cardiovascular conditioning in a number of other ways. For example, the cardiovascular machines that you will find at your local gym may be equipped with a "submaximal VO_2" test. This test is a measurement of how well the heart supplies oxygenated blood to the exercising muscles and how efficiently those muscles receive oxygen from the blood. This test is a good way to determine maximal oxygen uptake—that is, whether you are in good shape. If you're curious about this, check with a fitness trainer at your local gym or see a doctor for a checkup and stress test.

Find the Time

Why don't we exercise with more regularity and passion? Are we choosing exercises that are too repetitive or boring? Do they lack excitement or stimulation? Are they too monotonous? For some of us, there is simply not enough time in the day. For others it's the fear of being pushed beyond our comfort zone. But we all know that exercise is good for us and that our bodies thrive on it.

Clearly, on one level, cardiovascular exercise is hard and repetitive work. Quite often it is the very dread of this type of monotonous activity that causes us not to do it. But on another level, cardiovascular exercise can be *fun*.

The good news is that there are many *creative* ways to make this happen. Listening to music that motivates you can turn a dull workout into something more enjoyable. When choosing a gym, you want to lean toward one that plays the type of music you enjoy. Ernie and I will show you how you can make your cardiovascular exercise *short and simple* and as diverse as you want. It all depends on how hard you want to push yourself on any given day.

But you must take the first step. You must find the time.

What Kind of Training?

In order to condition your body aerobically you must first pick an exercise that you enjoy and do not find tedious. For some it may be spending twenty minutes on a treadmill while watching the evening news. For others it may be churning on a stationary bike while reading the newspaper. Of course, you can also choose a rowing machine, a stair climber, a jump rope, or even a game of tennis for your exercise. Something as simple as a brisk walk around your neighborhood or the local lake could be as beneficial as any piece of high-tech gym equipment.

Be creative. Cross-train. Use the stairs at your office or home. Seek exercise opportunities—they are all around you.

Remember that the best cardiovascular exercise is the exercise you enjoy the most. Ernie, as you know from reading his introduction, *hates* to run, so he plays tennis and trains on the stationary bike and stair climber. Then he uses the treadmill for his cooldown walk. If you have access to a treadmill, using it on various grades will prepare you for walking four hours on a hilly golf course.

Levels of Exercise: Low-Intensity (Fat-Burning), Aerobic, Anaerobic

Everyone has heard of aerobic exercise, and we all have some knowledge of how to train aerobically. Generally, **aerobic** training is continuous, rhythmic, sometimes vigorous exercise that elevates the heart rate for an extended period of time and utilizes oxygen in the process. Moderate- to higher-intensity aerobic training is for the more condi-tioned individual who trains at the top of—and slightly above—the target zone. Those of us who are in decent physical condition can train at this level.

A popular form of aerobic exercise is low-intensity "steady-state" exercise (keeping your heart rate elevated at the same level for an extended period), which utilizes fat as the primary source of fuel. This type of training is for those who are focused only on burning body fat, have a low fitness level, or are nursing an injury that prohibits them from performing more strenuous training.

When exercising in this zone, you should not feel like you are breathing heavily. You should be able to whistle a tune while you walk, bike, or jog slowly. For example, an invigorating thirty-minute walk on a treadmill early in the morning before breakfast will burn your fat at a very efficient rate.

Anaerobic training (high-intensity interval training) is a method of exercise for the high-performance person who wants to get into tip-top cardiovascular shape and really challenge themselves. This level of exercise builds up endurance for sports that require a constant amount of energy, such as basketball, tennis, or squash. A benefit of this training is that this zone burns a very high percentage of fat. Since "anaerobic" means "without the use of oxygen," fats and carbohydrates are your primary fuel sources. High-intensity exercise dramatically accelerates the heart rate and is not recommended for anyone with heart or respiratory problems, because it can elevate your heart rate to a dangerous level. The higher the intensity of the activity, the shorter the interval should be. This type of exercise causes your metabolic rate to stay elevated for a longer period of time when you are finished exercising.

The secret to making this exercise ritual fun is **interval training**—a method of training that utilizes alternating low to moderate intensities of exercise to achieve stress and recovery. This will enable you to train your heart more effectively than steady-state exercise.

Interval Training—Using the Target Heart Rate Zone

So what exactly is this concept of interval training? It is a fast and efficient way to get in shape. It varies the routine and adds excitement to the workout. Interval training is a key to simulating the ups and downs of life.

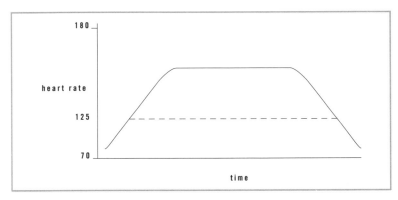

STEADY-STATE CURVE

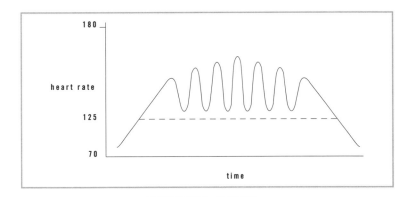

INTERVAL CURVE

Interval training means oscillating your heart rate by *speeding up* and *slowing down*. When speeding up you increase intensity and effort, creating what is referred to as the "cycle of stress." The slowing down is the reverse, the "cycle of rest and recovery."

This speeding up and slowing down is good for us because it mirrors life: the dash for the bus, the bolt up the steps to be on time for a meeting, the chase after the kids. The sudden stops. Life and golf (and most sports) move in spurts, and this form of training reflects that. Interval training permits a complete range of cardiovascular and fat-burning exercise.

Interval training can be performed throughout the high and low ends of your target heart rate zones by monitoring your heart rate by taking your pulse or using a heart rate monitor. This is the ideal exercise for individuals who are athletic achievers and for serious athletes who want to maximize and monitor their workout program and progress.

Those individuals with cardiovascular concerns, who may be exercising under a doctor's supervision, should begin with low-intensity aerobic activities.

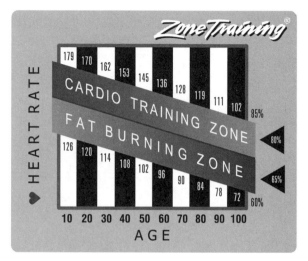

CALCULATING YOUR TARGET HEART RATE ZONE

A "target heart rate zone" (THRZ) chart appears on most cardiovascular exercise equipment. Let's start by explaining that small exercise chart on the exercise bike or treadmill. On most such pieces of equipment the charts look like the one above.

As you will notice, two separate zones are displayed: the "cardio training zone" and the "fat-burning zone." Ages are listed along the bottom of the chart. Use the following formula: 220, minus your age, multiplied by 65 percent and 85 percent. This formula is very conservative and safe. An experienced exerciser may find these zones fairly low for his or her level of fitness. These are safe zones for the novice exerciser or someone with potential health risks.

The target heart rate zone can also be calculated and explained in the following manner, using a fifty-year-old male for an example. To compute zones we will use the accepted target heart rate zone formula:

    220 − age [50] = maximum heart rate [170]
    × 65% = 110 beats per minute, or "bpm"
    × 85% = 145 bpm

The zone between 65 and 85 percent (110 to 145 bpm) is known as the target heart rate zone. The zone at 60 percent (102 bpm) is known as the fat-burning zone. Thus, for our fifty-year-old male:

- The **fat-burning** zone (60 percent of the maximum heart rate) is 102 bpm.
- The **aerobic** zone (65 percent to 85 percent) is 110 to 145 bpm.

FAT-BURNING ZONE

The fat-burning zone is low-intensity exercise below your aerobic zone. The primary source of fuel for the exercise is fat. If you exercise in this zone consistently during the early morning *before breakfast,* you will be able to reduce your body fat dramatically. Here's how:

Take a fat-burning walk, a slow run, or a moderate bike ride in the morning before breakfast. The goal is to elevate your heartbeat to 60 percent of your target heart rate (102 bpm if you are fifty years old) for twenty-five to thirty minutes. This means that you are generating a good sweat (if it's cold outside, wear a sweatshirt) so that you are causing a rise in your body-core temperature without heavy huffing and puffing. You are now beginning to create a fat-burning effect.

The reason for this is easy to understand. When we awaken, our bodies are in a fasting state where blood sugar and insulin levels are low. This is the best time to tap into stored body fat reserves for energy. This is why you exercise before eating breakfast. After a meal high in carbohydrates, blood sugar and insulin levels will rise in response to the food you are digesting, and fat burning will stop. Remember, however, that all the early-morning cardiovascular workouts you may perform will not get you the results you desire if you do not eat wisely the rest of the day.

AEROBIC ZONE

Many think that when they are training in the ranges of the aerobic zone they are burning a lot of fat. Unfortunately, this is not the case. Aerobics means training with oxygen as your primary source of fuel. The higher the intensity, the more you rely on carbohydrates for energy. Training in the aerobic zone is very beneficial for cardiorespiratory (cardiovascular) training, but not necessarily the most efficient way to burn fat.

OUTSIDE OF THE ZONE—THE ANAEROBIC WORKOUT

Anaerobic interval training means you are training above your heart rate zones. This is not for the novice exerciser. A checkup and a solid aerobic training base are highly recommended before engaging in anaerobic exercise. Your main sources of fuel are glycogen (carbohydrates) and fat. High-intensity anaerobic interval training gives you two benefits. Not only does it burn a higher amount of fat (thus burn more calories), but it will continue to burn calories after your workout is over by revving up your metabolism.

Remember that only people who are physically fit and have no cardiovascular concerns should exercise at this level.

AN INTERVAL WORKOUT FOR YOU

Let me give you examples of several interval workouts:

Biking

Most of us are familiar with the exercise bike. If you have back trouble, try the recumbent bike. Most bikes have a "Manual" mode, in which you can change the levels at any time and work out as vigorously or as casually as you desire. Many exercise bikes are now equipped with heart rate sensors that can be activated by holding on to a bar on the machine. If you do not have access to an exercise bicycle with a sensor, consider purchasing a heart rate monitor. They can be found at your local sporting goods store. A monitor is an excellent gauge to use for cardiovascular conditioning and will help you in your training. I would highly recommend getting one.

You can start by spinning the bike at Level 2, Manual for eight to ten minutes at 80 to 90 repetitions per minute (rpms), a steady-state aerobic warm-up. This will increase your heart rate and help prepare you mentally and physically for the workout. After the eight to ten minutes, evaluate how you feel and check your heart rate. You should be somewhere between the bottom and middle ranges of your target heart rate zone.

Switch to Level 5, Manual and spin at 110 to 120 rpms for forty-five seconds. Keep an eye on your heart rate and make sure it does not go above the top of your target heart rate zone. If after thirty seconds you hit the top zone, then immediately drop back down to Level 1 or 2, spin slowly, breathe deeply, and recover until you hit the lower end of your zone.

If it takes you two to three minutes to recover to the bottom range of your target heart rate zone, then you know you will need to start your program slowly and cautiously. If at Level 5 at 120 rpms for forty-five seconds you've hardly raised your heart rate and you recovered in thirty to forty-five seconds, then you are likely an avid exerciser and can work at higher-intensity interval training zones. Again, we stress that it is very important to get a checkup before starting any exercise program.

Outdoor Exercise

If you enjoy walking or jogging outdoors and don't have access to a gym, try warming up by walking briskly for ten minutes. Then walk fast for at least a minute (you judge how intense the interval should be) and then slow down. When you feel you've recovered, pick up the speed and take off again. Do these intervals for a minimum of ten to twenty minutes.

If you are a jogger, jog for eight to ten minutes. When you feel ready, accelerate your speed for thirty seconds to a minute. Slow down and jog or walk slowly again until you feel recovered. Repeat this exercise interval. Have fun with it, change the interval times, do three one-minute intervals, three forty-five-second intervals, and finish with three thirty-second intervals.

The same system can obviously be employed with any form of aerobic exercise. Again, the idea is to start at the lower end of your target heart rate zone, take your heart rate up (stress), and bring it back down (recovery).

SOME REMINDERS FOR YOUR WORKOUTS

You will feel whether you are ready for a low-, medium-, or high-intensity interval workout. Remember that intervals are doses of stress followed by immediate doses of recovery. A high-intensity workout means that you give yourself less time to recover between intervals or increase the level to create more stress to your system. Intervals can be performed for a shorter duration, such as ten seconds, or a longer duration, up to two minutes. Ten seconds is more anaerobic, whereas two minutes is more aerobic.

Your aim is to create stress and recovery by increasing your heart rate and teaching your body to recover fast. In the process, your overall aerobic fitness will improve by leaps and bounds. This will help you on the golf course and at the conference table.

UNDERSTANDING YOUR ENERGY LEVELS

If you feel abundant levels of energy or you feel extremely motivated, you can challenge yourself with a higher-intensity workout. Mentally you are connected and ready to push. Today, you might be thinking, "I'm going to take my fitness to the next level."

On the other hand, if you feel tired and sluggish, then you should have a light day or a maintenance day, when you reduce your level or amount of exercise. Maybe you had a tough day at work or didn't sleep well last night. No reason to go into the gym and overdo it. The key to having a consistent and progressive program is understanding your own feelings and body and knowing when to push and when not to. This comes through experience.

Cardiovascular conditioning is a key component not only in improving your score, but in enhancing your health and life. You will be more alert and focused, have more stamina, more pep, and an increased ability to alertly wrap up your work at the office and blaze out to the course for an evening round or hit the gym for your time-efficient workout.

Strengthen Your Body

*We want to get you ready and fit for golf. But be careful and don't
overdo it with heavy weights. You want to be fit enough to
walk eighteen holes comfortably and give it 100 percent on every shot.
That will make it easier to take some cash off your buddies.*

ERNIE ELS

Introduction

IN THIS CHAPTER WE WILL SHOW YOU how strength training can
be effectively and efficiently used to both enhance your general condition and improve
your golf game. You will see how a solid and consistent strength training program (often
called "resistance training") will help you:

- increase muscle tone

- enhance motor skill development

- prevent injuries

- add stamina

- increase the quality of your practice and play time

- make all aspects of your life and game more fit

We will establish a series of general and golf-specific strength-oriented workout routines that can be performed at the gym, at your home, at the office, and even when you travel. You can use these exercises to strengthen your weaker areas to improve your overall fitness and golf game. We will outline for you both a general conditioning regimen, as well as a golf-specific training program, which will focus on exercises that:

- develop better posture
- create muscular balance between the right and left sides of the body
- focus on the core muscles of the body (those principally involved in the swing: abdominals, obliques, lower back, hips)
- avoid overdeveloping areas of the body that could affect your swing and cause you to lose flexibility and speed
- take into consideration your past injuries and help prevent new ones

A powerful swing is the result of tension between your upper and lower body. You need to be strong in both your legs and your obliques to create balance and speed in your swing.

Golf-Specific Training

Strengthening your body for golf is quite different from strengthening it for any other sport. Fitness trainers use the term "golf-specific training." This means that you are conditioning and developing the muscles of your body that are involved in maintaining the proper setup and swing. These golf-specific exercises will also create more speed in your swing. Another benefit is increased muscle awareness, which will help you train your motor skills more effectively.

Golf-specific exercises are aimed at increasing your strength, your muscular endurance, your flexibility, and your overall conditioning where it's most important in the golf swing—particularly in the core muscles and lower body. Core strength and flexibility training are the keys to stabilizing the body, maintaining posture, and creating speed. When your instructor tells you to "move your body through the shot," he or she is referring to this core group of muscles. So focus on:

- protecting and supporting your lower back (the lumbar area of the spine)—a crucial factor when training
- avoiding exercises that stress your back and can potentially put unnecessary pressure on your spine—such as squats and dead lifts
- staying away from heavy weights in exercises that create uncomfortable soreness through the hamstrings, buttocks, lower back, and chest—such as lunges or bench presses
- using proper form and good athletic posture

Too much soreness in any area of your body can certainly affect your swing. For example, if you constantly do exercises with heavy weights that overwork the chest and shoulders (heavy chest presses, incline presses, military presses), then you are potentially tightening the chest and shoulders, which can cause restricted movement at the top of the backswing. If you perform too many heavy squats ("butt-loading" exercises), you could tighten up your glutes and restrict your turn. Imagine strolling through a round of golf with sore hamstrings and glutes. Not only would that be a continuing, nagging discomfort, but it would affect your swing because you might change your swing to avoid the discomfort.

This type of soreness may be inevitable if you're looking to become a bodybuilder, but it's totally counterproductive for golf. We are aiming to increase your

strength stamina. We don't want you to lift 250 pounds with one stupendous exertion, but instead to perform fifteen repetitions of 50 pounds for two, three, or four sets. This conditioning will build your endurance to allow you to be strong and finish strong at the end of your eighteen (or thirty-six) holes of weekend golf. Strength training will increase club head speed and you should hit the ball quite a few yards farther off the tee.

Additionally, while engaging in golf-specific exercise, keep in mind another important concept: **balance.** It is an essential ingredient to training and playing. You must work to develop both sides of your body. Some golf instructors have their students practice swinging from their opposite side. This switch-hitting or reverse-side golf swing exercise gives stability to your body's muscle tone and prevents overdeveloping (and overcompensating with) one side or portion of your body. It also increases flexibility—your range of motion—in your turn.

Strength in the chest, shoulders, triceps, and forearms is important for generating club head speed at impact.

There are also ways to promote balance in your body in the gym. Once in a while instead of doing your biceps exercises (curls) on a machine or with a barbell, try exercising your biceps individually with free weights. You will probably discover that one arm can lift more than the other. You are probably using that dominant arm more on the biceps machine. The dumbbells assure you that you are creating a balance of strength between your left and right sides. The same is true of leg extensions. Try them one leg at a time on the machine and you will find that one quad is weaker.

Additionally, this type of isolated activity will exercise all of your associated stabilizer muscles (when doing a dumbbell curl you will notice more use of your shoulder muscles). Don't let your dominant muscles prevail. Think balance:

- Balance your body—develop an equal amount of strength between the left and right sides of your body.
- Balance your exercise program—incorporate both general and golf-specific exercises into your workout.
- Balance your workout—switch from dumbbells to free weights to machines.
- Balance your intensity—go to fatigue, not to failure.

Understanding Your Program

As you can imagine, there are various theories regarding strength training for golf. Some trainers use heavier weights; some focus entirely on injury prevention. Our approach is to individualize your program to you. You must understand your body type and factor in your age, weight, goals, time, and your available facilities. One golfer might be content with his upper body strength but know he needs to develop his lower body and torso to stabilize his base. Another golfer might be less concerned with strength levels than he is with trimming his waistline.

Ernie's Program

When I work out I try to stay away from exercises that make me sore in the areas that affect my swing. Since my training program is often interrupted for up to three weeks, it is very easy to get sore the first day back in the gym. I always give myself at least two good workouts on each muscle group before I start to raise the intensity.

A key to strength training for golf is knowing that it is better to undertrain your body than to risk injury and soreness by overtraining. As a professional golfer, I do workouts consisting of three phases:

1. Preparation. This is a period when I am not playing any tournaments (my four-week layoff at the end of the year). My conditioning program is more intensive and I focus on general strength training exercises rather than on golf-specific training. Dave keeps a moderate level of soreness in my targeted muscle groups—this increases my strength and stamina. This is a good time to rebuild my cardiovascular base and focus on rehabilitating any injured areas.

2. Active. This phase lasts from seven to fourteen days between tournaments and varies with my playing schedule and travel. During this time I normally get two to three days of strength training per week, combin-

Strength alone is not enough. Having flexible muscles and joints is another way to enhance power in your swing.

ing both general and golf-specific exercises. Here, I aim to strengthen and protect the areas of my body susceptible to injury; create a comfortable level of muscle soreness in areas (such as my quads) that will not affect my swing; and concentrate on my core exercises. I also focus on my cardiovascular work.

3. Competitive. This is the maintenance phase I use while I am playing tournaments. On Monday and Tuesday I do light golf-specific toning exercises. On Wednesday I work on core strengthening exercises and every day I stretch, focusing on my hips, hamstrings, and lower back. During the four days of a tournament I will try to jump on the bike twice for a light workout and stretch.

Your Program

Your strength program must be progressive, achievable, and centered on what you enjoy doing most. Dave has set forth a detailed series of exercises for **general** and **golf-specific** strengthening. The general exercises are to get you started and improve your overall fitness. They will help you to develop a base of strength that you'll need to keep your body balanced as you advance to the golf-specific exercises. Once you feel comfortable with these exercises, we suggest you start incorporating the golf-specific exercises into your routine. You can select your comfort zone and design your own workouts. Keep in mind the following:

*   When starting an exercise, always do a warm-up set first.
*   Each exercise set should be performed for twelve to twenty repetitions, bringing about muscle fatigue—not muscle strain—toward the end of each set.
*   Proper breathing rhythm is important—exhale while exerting, do not hold your breath (this could elevate your blood pressure).
*   Each exercise should be performed repetitively for one to four sets.
*   Include cardiovascular exercises for maximum aerobic and fat-burning benefits.
*   Stretch after your workout or after each set.

GENERAL TRAINING EXERCISES
Upper Body Strengthening Exercises

Dumbbell Chest Press

Lie on your back on a bench, holding a dumbbell in each hand. With your elbows out to your sides and your palms facing forward, slowly lower the dumbbells to a point just above your shoulders (Figure 1). Press the weights up and toward each other until they slightly touch, making a triangular shape with your arms (Figure 2). Slowly lower the weights back to the starting position.

NOTES

- There is also a machine equivalent for this exercise. We don't recommend doing a traditional straight bar bench press because it can potentially harm the shoulder joint.

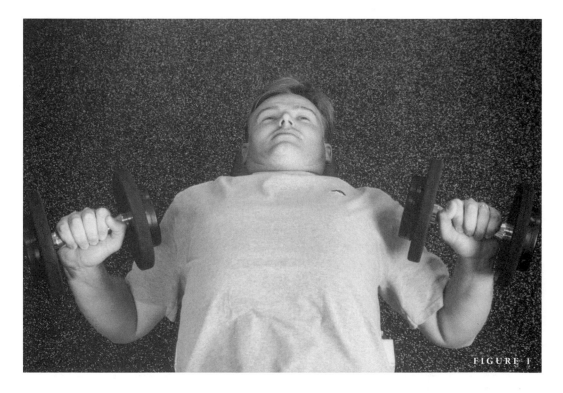

FIGURE 1

- Be sure to breathe out as you exert, and breathe in as you return to the starting position.
- Do not arch your back while performing the exercise.

Benefit: The chest press is a fundamental exercise in any strength training program. It is one of the basic exercises used to increase upper body strength and power.

FIGURE 2

Dumbbell Shoulder Press

Sit on a bench with a back support so you can maintain proper spinal alignment. Hold a dumbbell in each hand, at shoulder height, elbows out, with palms facing your ears (Figure 1). Press the dumbbells up, rotating your palms outward until the dumbbells touch slightly at the top, keeping your elbows slightly bent at the top of the movement (Figure 2). Slowly lower the weights to their starting position. Make sure to keep your chin level with the ground, and try not to bend your neck forward or backward while performing the repetitions.

NOTES

- You can do this exercise with dumbbells or on a machine, but dumbbells used correctly are safer on the shoulder than machines.
- Be sure to breathe out as you exert; breathe in as you return to the starting position.

FIGURE 1

• Be very careful not to let the weights sway back and forth, and avoid doing this exercise if you're experiencing any shoulder pain.

Benefit: This is another fundamental exercise that will help develop upper body strength.

FIGURE 2

Seated Lat Row

Sit on the machine with your chest pressed against the pad and your feet planted firmly on the floor. Reach forward and grasp the handles (Figure 1). From this position, pull your arms back, keeping them close to the sides of your body until your elbows are straight down and by your sides. Your back should maintain a natural arch, and your chest should stick out (Figure 2). With your arms as relaxed as possible (to keep tension on your lats), slowly release the weight to the starting position.

NOTES

- This exercise can be done with a machine, dumbbells, or cables.

FIGURE 1

- Pick a comfortable weight and begin with 1 or 2 sets; increase sets to 3 or 4 over several weeks.
- Avoid high-risk spinal curvature to reduce the chance of lower back injury.
- If you experience chronic lower back pain, you might want to avoid this exercise.

Benefit: This exercise strengthens a major muscle group of the upper body: the back. It's important for the muscles of the upper back, as well as the numerous muscle groups that help to support proper posture.

FIGURE 2

Lat Pull-Down

Sit at a lat pull-down machine and tuck your legs securely under the pads with your feet on the floor. Firmly grab the **V** handlebar (Figure 1). Keeping your neck and back straight, slowly pull the bar straight down to the top of your chest. Arch your back slightly as you pull the weight down to the bottom and position for a one-count (Figure 2). Slowly release the weight to the starting position.

NOTES

- For an alternative, you can use a wide-grip bar instead of a **V**-grip.
- Do not lock your elbows at the top. You should always maintain a slight flex to keep resistance on your lats throughout the movement.
- Don't overdo the weight. Using too much weight can create a lot of width in your upper back, which can potentially restrict your swing turn. Think light weight, high reps.

Benefit: Another exercise that can be great for developing and toning the lats if you're careful not to use too much weight.

FIGURE 1

FIGURE 2

Triceps Press-Down

Standing with your feet shoulder width apart, grasp the bar, making sure to keep your hands about 10 inches apart. Keep your elbows locked close to your body (Figure 1). Press the bar down to a locked-out position with your arms fully extended (Figure 2). Release the bar and let it come up to the point where the elbows are at 90 degrees. Throughout the exercise, maintain a flexed, tight abdominal to help support the body.

NOTES

- Keep the shoulders back and together, creating a natural arch in the back. Avoid any movement of the shoulders during this exercise to isolate the triceps.
- Slowly press down until the bar slightly touches your upper thighs.
- Occasionally reverse your grip to work a slightly different area of the triceps.

> **Benefit:** This is a basic upper arm exercise that strengthens the back of the arm and increases the muscular tone and strength of the triceps. This exercise helps to protect your elbow from overuse injuries.

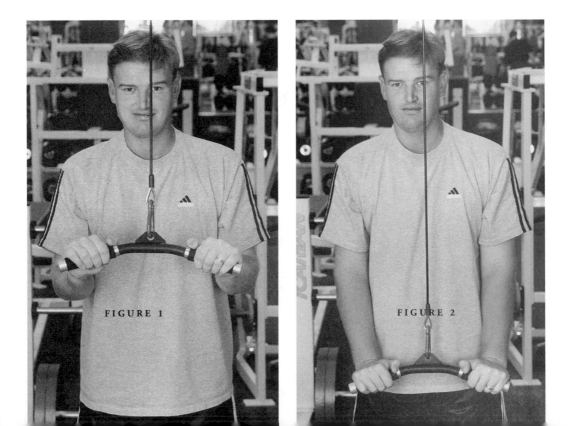

FIGURE 1   FIGURE 2

Dumbbell Biceps Curl

Sit on the edge of a flat bench or a bench with a back support. Position your arms down at your sides, your palms facing forward and a dumbbell in each hand (Figure 1). Curl one arm at a time toward your shoulder (Figure 2). At the top of the movement, flex the muscle and then slowly lower your arm to the starting position, keeping tension on the muscle throughout the exercise. Repeat the process with your other arm.

NOTES

• For a variation, alternate between doing this exercise with dumbbells, barbells, and machines.

FIGURE 1

- Do not rock back and forth while performing this exercise. If you do tend to sway, try placing your upper back against a wall.
- Be careful not to overdo this exercise the first few workout sessions, or you run a real risk of severe muscle soreness or even injury.

Benefit: This exercise helps balance the strength between the front and back of the arm.

FIGURE 2

Lower Body Strengthening Exercises

Leg Press

Sit in the machine so that your lower back is positioned firmly against the backrest. Place your feet in full contact with the crosspiece (Figure 1). As you grasp the safety handles, straighten your legs to support the weight (Figure 2). Release the safety bars and slowly lower the weight, keeping your knees in line with your shoulders. Press the weight up until your knees are almost straight, but do not lock them. Be careful not to lower to the point where your lower back lifts off the backrest.

FIGURE 1

NOTES

- Concentrate on keeping your back supported and flat throughout the exercise.
- With lighter weights, focus on the fronts of the quads (thighs) by keeping the resistance primarily on the balls of the feet.
- With heavier weights, do not lift your heels off the platform, as this potentially causes knee problems.

Benefit: This is a good all-purpose exercise for quads, hamstrings, and glutes. It's also an excellent exercise to increase lower body strength and power, as it develops many muscle groups of the upper leg and hip.

FIGURE 2

Leg Extension

Sit on the machine with your back straight and roller pads positioned so they rest on the bottoms of your shins. Hook your ankles under the roller pads, grasping the handles for balance and support (Figure 1). Extend your legs outward, keeping a slight bend in your knees (Figure 2). Slowly return to the starting position.

NOTES

- Try doing one set with your toes pointed out (duck-toed), one set with your toes pointed in (pigeon-toed), and one set with your toes pointed forward. Each angle works a different muscle of the quadriceps.

FIGURE 1

- For a variation, try this exercise using one leg at a time, putting all the resistance and focus on one leg. Remember to lower the weight.
- Avoid bringing the leg down below a 90-degree angle.
- Avoid locking out the knees at the top of the movement.
- Avoid fast and jerky movements.
- If you feel any hint of pain in the knee, stop or decrease the weight.

Benefit: This exercise directly strengthens the quadriceps (thigh) muscles of the upper leg. Stronger legs allow you to lead a more active lifestyle and participate in athletic activities without getting as tired. This is also an excellent exercise to strengthen the muscles that help support and protect the knees.

FIGURE 2

Leg Curl

Lie facedown on the machine and hook your heels under the roller pads. Hold on to the handles or the bench itself for support (Figure 1). Press your pelvis down and pull your lower legs up until they form a 90-degree angle with your upper leg (Figure 2). Relax the feet and stabilize your body with your trunk muscles. Slowly lower the legs down to the starting position.

NOTES

- Again, try doing one set with your toes pointed out (duck-toed), one set with your toes pointed in (pigeon-toed), and one set with your toes pointed forward. Each angle works a different muscle of the hamstrings.

FIGURE 1

- This is an excellent warm-up exercise before stretching the hamstrings.
- Alternate workouts with single-leg curls.
- Make sure you use a light to moderate weight on this exercise.
- To minimize stress on the lower back, keep your hips pressed down against the bench as you perform this exercise.

Benefit: Well-conditioned and supple hamstrings help to prevent lower back pain and improve performance by providing muscular balance in the upper leg.

FIGURE 2

Standing Calf Raise

Place your shoulders under the pads of the machine, and adjust your feet so that the balls of your feet are on the step. Keeping your legs straight, lower your heels as far as possible, creating a deep stretch in the calf muscle (Figure 1). Then raise your legs as high as possible (Figure 2). Pause momentarily at the top, and slowly lower to the stretched position.

NOTES

- Begin with 1 set and minimal weight, keeping your repetitions around 20. If you're not feeling a strong burn at 20, then try squeezing the calves hard at the top of the contraction.

FIGURE 1

- As you advance, increase the weight and build up to 3 sets of 20 repetitions.
- Vary the position of your feet as in the previous exercises. Each angle will work a different area of the upper calf.
- Be careful. Your calves can become very sore after the first few workouts.

Benefit: Strong calf muscles help by providing balance and power in the lower body.

FIGURE 2

Core Strengthening Exercises

Lower Ab Tilt with Bench

Lie on a bench on your back with your hands anchored over your head. Raise your knees and feet slightly off the bench so that your lower back is flat against the bench (Figure 1). Begin the exercise by rolling the pelvis and legs upward until the muscles in the lower abdominals are fully contracted (Figure 2). Slowly lower to the starting position on a 5-second count.

NOTES

- Be sure to squeeze your knees together and keep your toes pointed down.
- Be careful not to roll past full abdominal contraction, as this can put excess stress on your neck.
- Be sure not to rock back past the starting position, as this puts stress on your lower back.

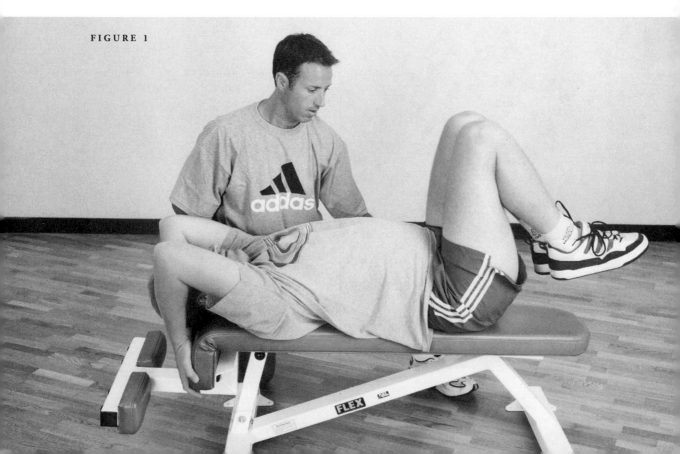

FIGURE 1

- Begin with 1 or 2 sets; do as many repetitions as you can until your abs burn.
- It could take you three or four workout days to get the technique correct for this exercise. After that, consult a personal trainer if you're not feeling the burn in your lower abdominals.
- If you're feeling pressure in your neck, then you are doing the exercise incorrectly.

Benefit: This is a key core exercise for trunk stabilization. This exercise strengthens the lower abdominals, which help to support and protect the lower back.

Dave helps me with my form. Always feel free to ask a trainer if you have a question about how to do a certain exercise.

FIGURE 2

Upper Ab Curl

Lie on the floor on your back with your knees raised and your feet flat on the floor, close to your buttocks. Keeping your lower back pressed firmly against the floor, contract the abdominal muscles and pull the rib cage up and toward the pelvis (Figures 1 and 2). Hold for 2 seconds and maintain tension while you breathe out. Slowly lower your body to the starting position, never releasing the tension from the abdominals. Repeat.

FIGURE 1

NOTES

- Make sure to keep your head and neck in a neutral position.
- Begin with 2 sets and perform as many repetitions as you can.

Benefit: Another key core exercise, this upper ab strengthener will help to tone your stomach and support and protect your back from injury.

FIGURE 2

Hyperextension

Stand on the platform of the machine with your feet placed directly in line with your legs. Cross your arms in front of you and slowly lower your upper body while maintaining a natural arch in your lower back (Figure 1). Stop at 45 degrees (Figure 2) and, squeezing your lower back muscles, bring your body back to its starting position (Figure 3). You also might feel your hamstrings and glutes contracting.

NOTES

- Be sure to perform this exercise slowly. Don't bounce.
- Begin with 1 set of 15 repetitions and progress to 1 set of 30.
- Extend your arms straight overhead for increased resistance.
- Be sure to perform this exercise slowly and smoothly.

FIGURE 1

Benefit: These will help you to strengthen your lower back muscles to prevent common muscular strains that can occur in everyday activities.

FIGURE 2

FIGURE 3

Figure 3 is an example of bad form. Your spine should never extend back past your legs during Hyperextensions.

GOLF-SPECIFIC FITNESS EXERCISES

These exercises focus on the muscles used in the mechanics of the golf swing. These muscle groups also need to be strengthened to prevent future injuries that can occur when practicing or playing.

Keep in mind that you should be seeking:

- lower body strength and power to stabilize your base
- trunk stabilization and core strength to create balance and increase rotational speed through the swing
- specific strengthening to create speed and power in your swing
- upper body toning and strengthening to help control the club

Remember: You must protect the spine in all of these exercises, and do not push yourself into unnecessary muscle soreness. As you'll see in the workout programs, for an even better effect, make sure to stretch between sets and at the end of the workout.

Note: Golf-fit benefit descriptions are given for right-handed players.

Golf-Fit Upper Body Exercises

Chest Fly

Sit on the machine with your feet planted firmly on the floor. Set the machine so that your shoulders and arms are parallel to the set of handles (Figure 1). Turn and grasp the right handle and bring it to the midpoint of your body. As you hold at midpoint, turn and grasp the left handle and bring it also to the midpoint of your body (Figure 2). Slowly release both handles until your arms are directly at your sides. You should feel a stretch in your chest. Squeeze your chest muscles, returning both handles to the midpoint of your body.

NOTES

- On the last repetition, slowly let the weight back until you feel a stretch, then hold the stretch for a slow 10-to-20-second count.

- This exercise should not cause deep muscular soreness if performed within your limits.
- Do 1 or 2 sets of 12 to 20 repetitions.
- Squeeze your elbows and wrists together to get a full contraction.

Golf-fit benefit: The chest muscles are important for driving the arms through the ball at impact.

FIGURE 2

FIGURE 1

Straight Arm Pull

Sit on the machine with your arms held straight out in front of you and your hands on the handles (Figure 1). Without bending your elbows or arms, retract your shoulders, squeezing your shoulder blades together (Figure 2). Slowly release your shoulders back to the starting position.

NOTES

- The handles should move a maximum of four inches.
- Make sure to use very light weight on this exercise.

FIGURE 1

Golf-fit benefit: This is an excellent exercise for your posture. It also helps to strengthen the muscles that pull the right arm down on your downswing.

FIGURE 2

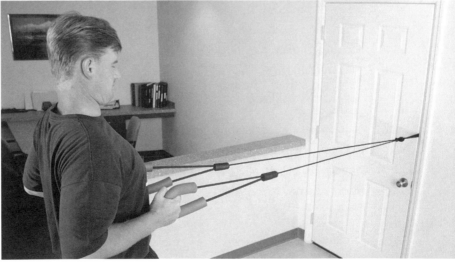

Another good way to exercise this part of the body is to do this variation of the Seated Lat Row (page 54) movement, but with an exercise band, as I'm doing here.

Dumbbell Lateral Raise

Stand holding your dumbbells, with your feet shoulder width apart. Bend your knees slightly, keeping a natural arch in the back. Your elbows should be slightly in front of your body and flexed at a 90-degree angle (Figure 1). Slowly raise your elbows and the weights simultaneously until they are parallel with your shoulders. Notice how the wrist, elbow, and shoulder are directly in one line (Figure 2). Be careful not to rotate your shoulder externally as you raise the dumbbells.

FIGURE 1

NOTES

- This is an excellent shoulder strengthening exercise because it requires light weight and does not put excess stress on the shoulder joint.
- This strengthening exercise is also used to help protect the muscles of the rotator cuff.
- Do 1 or 2 sets of 15 to 20 repetitions.
- Stay away from heavier weighted dumbbells (above 12 pounds).

Golf-fit benefit: The shoulder muscles are used to help elevate the arms during the backswing. Strong shoulder muscles also help to control the club at the top of the swing.

Notice the symmetry between the shoulder, elbow, and wrist.

FIGURE 2

Rear Deltoid Fly

Sit facing the machine with your feet placed firmly on the floor. Adjust the height of the machine so that your shoulders are the same height as the handles. Reach forward and grasp the handles (Figure 1). Contract the muscles of the back of the shoulder while squeezing your shoulder blades together (Figure 2). Then, slowly release back to the starting position, constantly keeping tension on the muscle.

NOTES

- Do 1 or 2 sets of 12 to 15 repetitions.
- Be careful to use light weight—this is crucial for preventing shoulder strains during exercise.

Golf-fit benefit: This exercise develops the back of the shoulder, which helps protect your rotator cuff. It also strengthens the muscle group that helps decelerate the club during your follow-through.

FIGURE 1

FIGURE 2

Golf-Fit Arm
Strengthening Exercises

(Please also refer to Forearm Supination and Pronation on page 133.)

Rope Triceps Press-Down

Stand with your feet shoulder width apart, holding a rope. Grasp the rope handle and keep your hands about 8 to 10 inches apart. Your arms should be locked and close to your body (Figure 1). Press the rope down, fully extending the arms, locking out your elbows in a triangular position (Figure 2). Slowly release the rope, constantly keeping tension on the muscle as you return to your starting position.

NOTES

- Most gyms have ropes to use for this exercise.
- Maintain a flexed, tight abdomen to help support the body throughout the movement.

> *Golf-fit benefit:* The stronger your triceps, the quicker you can straighten out your right arm on the downswing.

FIGURE 1

FIGURE 2

Forearm Curl

Stand with your feet shoulder width apart and your knees slightly flexed (Figure 1). With your palms facing down, begin the exercise by raising the EZ curl bar until it is even with your shoulders (Figure 2). Slowly lower the bar to the starting position.

NOTES

- Cables or dumbbells can also be used (see page 132).
- Make sure that your upper arm remains locked at your side and that you are bending at the elbows, not raising your shoulders.

Golf-fit benefit: This is an excellent exercise to help create forearm strength and prevent potential elbow problems. It's important to have strong forearms to hit balls that are deep in the rough and to protect the elbows and wrists from overuse injuries.

FIGURE 1   FIGURE 2

Golf-Fit Trunk Exercises Using Balls and Bands

Reverse Ab Tilt with Ball

Lie flat on your back on the floor with your legs placed over a ball. Place your arms firmly on the floor, palms down (Figure 1). Grab the ball with both legs and begin the exercise with the ball slightly off the floor, keeping tension in your abdominal muscles. Make sure your head and neck stay flat on the floor. Contract your lower abdominals, pulling the pelvis toward the rib cage (Figure 2). Hold the position for 2 seconds and slowly lower the ball to its starting position using a 5-second count.

NOTES

- Be careful not to roll past full abdominal contraction, as this can put excess stress on your neck.
- Be sure not to rock back past your starting position, as this puts stress on the lower back.
- Begin with 1 or 2 sets, and do as many repetitions as you can until your abs burn.
- It could take three or four workout days to get the technique correct for this exercise. After that, consult a personal trainer if you're not feeling the burn in your lower abdominals.
- If you're feeling pressure in your neck, then you are doing the exercise incorrectly.

Golf-fit benefit: This exercise strengthens the lower abdominals, which help support the lower back. This is one of the best exercises to help develop the muscles that stabilize your trunk during your golf swing.

FIGURE 1

FIGURE 2

Upper Ab Curl with Ball

Lie on the Exerball on your back with your arms crossed and your feet planted firmly on the floor. Spread your legs so that your knees are placed slightly wider than your shoulders (Figure 1). With the shoulders just higher than the hips and your pelvis pressed firmly against the ball, contract the abdominals, raising your trunk up and off the ball (Figure 2). Hold for 2 seconds and return to the starting position.

NOTES

- Keep your head and neck in a neutral position.
- Begin with 1 or 2 sets and perform 15 repetitions each.
- It is better to place your arms across your chest or under your chin than behind your head.

Golf-fit benefit: Strong abdominal muscles are important in supporting the twisting and turning that occurs during the golf swing.

FIGURE 1

FIGURE 2

Diagonal Trunk Rotation with Band

Holding an exercise band, lie on your back with your knees up and your feet flat on the floor. With both arms extended over your right shoulder, grasp the band with both hands (Figure 1). In a twisting diagonal motion, lift your right shoulder off the ground and extend your arms toward your left knee, pause for 2 seconds, and slowly lower to the starting position (Figure 2). Then switch the angle of your body so that both arms are extended over your left shoulder. Repeat.

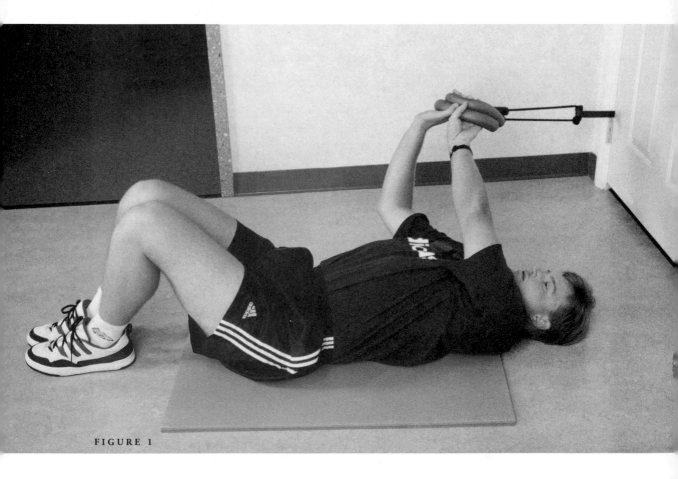

FIGURE 1

NOTES

- Squeeze and contract your obliques (the muscles on the sides of your abs) to create the movement. Don't use your shoulders to pull the band across your body.
- Focus on touching your right shoulder to the opposite left and vice versa.
- The challenge here is keeping tension in your obliques throughout the exercise, especially as you lower yourself to the starting position.

Golf-fit benefit: Your obliques fire on the downswing, helping to accelerate your shoulders so that they catch up to your hips at impact. Strong obliques help create speed in your swing.

FIGURE 2

Lower Back Hyperextension on Ball

Lie stomach-down on the ball with your knees slightly flexed, legs spread apart, and feet flush against the wall. Place your arms next to your body or overhead, depending on the resistance you desire (Figure 1). Begin with your trunk slightly flexed and your pelvis pressed firmly against the ball. Contract your lower back muscles to raise your upper body up and off the ball (Figure 2). Hold for 2 seconds, and then slowly lower to the starting position.

NOTES

- Raise your head, shoulders, and chest off the ball by squeezing the muscles of the lower back.
- Be sure to squeeze your shoulder blades together as you hold for 2 seconds.
- Notice how the body is fully stretched out.
- Keep your head and neck in a neutral position.
- For more resistance, extend your arms forward overhead.
- This is an area of the body that you do not want to overdevelop or overtrain, so 1 or 2 sets should be plenty of work on this muscle group.

Golf-fit benefit: Strengthening the lower back muscles will allow you to practice your putting for longer periods of time without tiring. Having fit and toned lower back muscles can also help prevent a potential injury. Weak lower back muscles make it difficult to obtain good posture.

FIGURE 1

FIGURE 2

Golf-Fit Lower Body Strengthening Exercises

(Note: The general lower body exercises all have excellent golf-specific benefits.)

Exerball Wall Squat

Stand with your back against a wall, with an Exerball positioned behind the lower part of your back. With your knees slightly bent, position your feet slightly in front of your body, shoulder width apart (Figure 1). Slowly lower yourself into a sitting position, allowing the ball to roll up your back (Figure 2). Pause for a moment and return to the starting position. Be careful not to bend your legs beyond a 90-degree angle.

FIGURE 1

NOTES

- This is an excellent exercise for the upper leg.
- Make sure to place the ball at the lower part of your back.
- As you descend you should feel the ball roll up your back.
- Begin with 1 or 2 sets of 12 to 20 repetitions, and advance to 3 sets.

FIGURE 2

Golf-fit benefit: Strong legs are extremely important for anchoring the lower body. They support the rotation of your trunk and enable you to create more speed as you turn.

Hip Adduction

Sit at the machine with your back in a neutral position against the backrest. Place your feet in the ankle supports and the insides of your knees against the leg pads (Figure 1). In a smooth motion, squeeze your legs together, pause for 2 seconds, then return to the starting position (Figure 2).

NOTES

- Begin with 1 light set of 15 to 20 repetitions.
- You can use an Exerball for this movement. Just squeeze the ball with your

FIGURE 1

knees and inner thighs and hold for 3 seconds. Release slowly and repeat 10 to 15 times.

- Be sure not to overdo this exercise the first few workouts, as this muscle can easily become sore.

Golf-fit benefit: The inner thigh helps to stabilize your lower body and torso. It also helps fire the right hip (thigh) into the left leg, creating a more explosive hip turn.

FIGURE 2

Hip Abduction

Sit at the machine with your back in a neutral position against the backrest. Place your feet in the ankle supports and the outsides of the knees against the leg pads (Figure 1). In a smooth motion, push legs as far as is comfortable, pause for 2 seconds, then return to the starting position (Figure 2).

FIGURE 1

FIGURE 2

NOTES

• This strengthens the muscles on the outsides of the hips.

• You can be a little more aggressive adding weight here because you're less likely to get sore than with the adduction.

• Start with 1 or 2 sets of 15 to 20 repetitions.

Golf-fit benefit: Strong hips help create lower body stabilization and power throughout the golf swing. The left hip helps stabilize the left leg. At impact, the left leg is the axis at which the entire body unwinds.

CHAPTER SIX

Flexibility

Stretch for Success

*Whatever it takes, this is important. Without suppleness and torque,
all you will do is punch the golf ball. For rhythm, rotation, and results,
you need to be flexible. Stretching, especially as we age, is crucial. So whatever it
takes—the gym, yoga, massage—you have to dedicate yourself.
Be limber, be loose—you have no excuse!*

ERNIE ELS

Introduction

HOW IMPORTANT IS FLEXIBILITY? To me, it is—without any doubt—the key factor in my golf swing. If you lack the flexibility to properly wind up your body, you will never get the distance you desire nor the satisfaction you deserve. Becoming more flexible will ease your stiff back, loosen up your hamstrings, release your hip flexors, enhance your posture, relax your body, and lower your handicap. Additionally, as Dave reminds me—sharing an experience of one of his older clients— flexibility will improve your circulation, decreasing the likelihood of degenerative diseases.

My swing coach, Robert Baker, says the following about flexibility:

> You must be flexible to have good technique. No doubt about it. The stronger and more flexible your hips and shoulders are and the more aware of your balance you are, the better a player you will be. If you are not flexible in certain areas, it can force your body to move out of balance or out of position to get the club in the right slot. Often I have corporate clients who can only turn their shoulders 5 degrees when seated in a chair. But I also have players who can rotate 90 degrees sitting down! If you are flexible you can get in position easier without as much manipulation. For example, many people have the simple problem of not being able to properly cock the wrist and keep the left arm straight. Others just can't simply turn their shoulders or rotate their hips.

Many players cannot wind up properly, so their legs will slide to the side to overcompensate. Having flexible hips and back is very important. A controlled hip turn with a big shoulder rotation creates a bigger differential between the hips and shoulder, creating more coil and more power.

Keep in mind that the older you are, the less flexibility you have. Adhesions form around the muscles. These adhesions can form through a variety of ways—old sports injuries, lifting heavy weights, and trauma to specific areas of the body. By stretching on a regular and consistent basis (along with other helpful methods, such as massage and heat) you can get these adhesions to release. Stretching can promote the production of lubricants between the connective tissue fibers, which helps to prevent these adhesions.

Is there a fun way to stretch? Not for me! But we can be creative and seek ways to improve our flexibility. Stretch while you are watching the evening news. Do a series of stretches while you are on the plane or train. Twist your body while awaiting the second half of the game or play or concert. Get a personal "stretcher" or find a flexibility class at your gym. Try yoga. Find a good masseur. The key is to be aware of the possibilities. The following is both practical and enjoyable.

Massage

Massage—now that's a pleasant way to train and a great way to increase your flexibility. Intense and rigorous exercise puts stress on your body. Exercise and stress can actually lead to thickening connective tissue, thereby making you more rigid. A massage helps your flexibility because the pressure, friction, and stretching all heat up and loosen that tissue. If you have scar tissue, collagen fibers form a weave to repair tissue damage and tighten the tissue. The massage breaks down the adhesions that restrict the range of motion. Additionally, massage can increase the removal of cellular waste such as lactic acid, which speeds recovery time, thus boosting muscular energy.

Consider one of the wide range of massage options, from sport to shiatsu. It feels good and is helpful, a rare combination!

General Stretching Guidelines

Dave has introduced me to twelve stretches that can be performed anywhere. Each of them serves a very specific purpose and is useful and effective *if* you have the discipline and patience to persevere. Stretching is *progressive.* You have to stay at it or you backslide.

Here are our general guidelines:
- Stretch before you tee off. Build in the time for this, for if you rush, you are likely to start your round off poorly.
- Hold the stretch for at least fifteen seconds but up to a full minute—feel the gentle pull and release. Each stretch should be done one to three times.
- During your stretch, feel free to slightly change angles to find other tight areas within the same muscle groups.
- While playing, keep stretching, and breathe deeply and rhythmically as you stretch.
- Make stretching part of your everyday routine.

My dad loves to run, but he refuses to stretch. He can't and won't bend. This is not healthy over the long term. You can stretch at the office while sitting or standing. Create ways to limber your body while you are idle. Do the stretches several times. And if you find stretching boring, by all means watch TV or listen to music.

Stretches

Here is what we recommend for your stretching routine. These exercises can be used in a gym, at home, in the office, or on the golf course. The key is to use them.

Chest Stretch

Stand upright, facing a pole. Extend your left arm, placing the open palm of your left hand against the pole. Slowly turn your upper body away from your arm. A thorough stretch should be felt in the chest, biceps, and shoulder. Repeat with the other arm.

Lat Stretch

Standing with your feet shoulder width apart, grasp a bar with your right arm. Sit back, slowly shifting your weight to your right side and right leg. Repeat for the other lat. Be careful not to hold the bar so low that it puts excess stress on your lower back.

Bent-Over Shoulder Stretch

Stand with your left side next to a pole. Bend over from your waist while grasping the pole with your right hand. Allow your body to lean against your right arm, feeling the stretch along the arm and back of the shoulder. Use your left hand to push against the pole to assist with the stretch. Repeat for your other shoulder.

Hamstring Stretch

Stand upright with one leg raised and resting on the bar of the Smith machine. Keep both legs straight and keep your hips squared to the bar. Bend forward from the waist while maintaining the natural arch in the back. Exhale and repeat for your other leg.

Challenge yourself by elevating the bar of the Smith machine to the next height, but be careful not to push yourself too far.

Quad Stretch

Set the bar of the Smith machine so that it is slightly lower than your hips. Stand upright, facing away from the bar. Place your left foot behind you, on the bar, and grasp the bar with both hands for support and balance. Slowly bend your right leg, keeping your chest and head up. Repeat for your other leg.

Glute Stretch

Set the bar of the Smith machine so that it is at the height of your hips. Stand upright facing the machine. Place your right knee, ankle, and foot on the bar. Position yourself so that the right foot is in line with the left hip. As you slowly lean into the stretch, maintaining a natural arch in your back, make sure your right foot stays in line with the left elbow and hip. Repeat for the other leg.

Hip Flexor Stretch

Lie on your back with your feet flat on the floor and your knees bent. Place your hands out to your sides, palms facing the ground. Place your left ankle on your right knee, allowing the weight of the left leg to push the right to the floor. A stretch should be felt along the right hip and in the lower back. Repeat for the other leg.

Hip Adductor Stretch

Sit upright on the floor. Bring the heels and soles of your feet together and pull them toward your buttocks. Place your elbows on the insides of both knees. Lean your upper body forward, maintaining a natural arch in your lower back. Slowly and gently push your legs to the floor. Breathe rhythmically as you stretch.

Lower Back Rotational Stretch

Lie flat on the floor with your legs extended and your arms stretched out, so that the body forms a T. Raise the right knee so that the right foot is beside the left knee. Gently pull the right knee across the body, keeping the right shoulder and right arm flat against the floor. As tension increases, relax into the stretch. Repeat the exercise for the other side.

In the photo, Dave is helping me, but when doing this exercise yourself, pull the right knee across the body using your left hand, and vice versa.

Upper Back Rotational Stretch

Lie on your right side. Bend your knees to form a 90-degree angle with your upper body. With each hand, grasp the opposite elbow (Figure 1). Turn your upper body in a twisting motion to the left (Figure 2). Relax into the stretch while exhaling at the sticking point. Inhale as you return to the starting position and repeat seven to ten times. Switch to your other side. Be aware of keeping your lower body firmly positioned against the floor. Do not raise your right hip off the floor during the twisting motion.

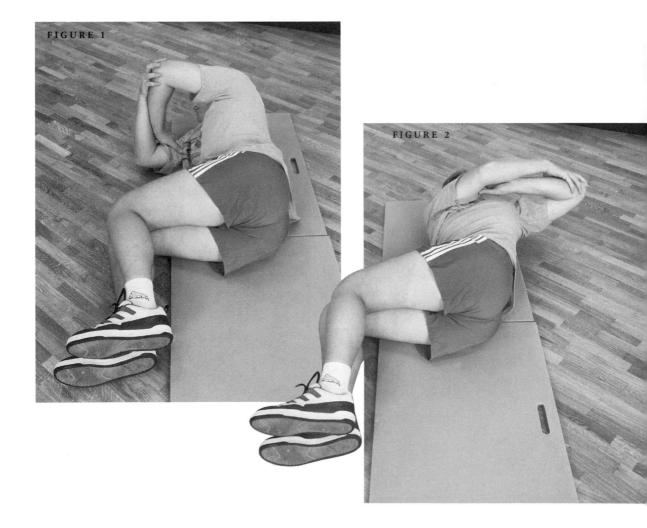

FIGURE 1

FIGURE 2

Hanging Lat Stretch (optional)

Grasp a stationary, overhead bar, placing your hands slightly wider than shoulder width apart. Relax and allow yourself to let go of all your body weight, feeling the stretch from your wrists, down into the forearms and biceps, through the shoulders and the upper back. Try to hold this stretch for 5 to 10 seconds. Use the floor for support, if necessary.

Lying Hamstring Stretch with Towel (optional)

Lie flat on your back, placing a towel around your right foot. Keeping your right leg straight, pull it up and toward your head. Be sure to keep your left leg and hip flat on the floor. Pull your right leg back to a comfortable position, and hold. Repeat for the other leg. Try to stay relaxed by breathing deeply and rhythmically during the stretch.

Injuries

Prevention and Relief

The opportunity for injury on the range or on the golf course is, unfortunately, far greater than you think, especially for the corporate golfer. Lack of conditioning, poor technique, early-season eagerness, advancing age, and inflexibility all contribute to the risk of injury. Work at avoiding it. Weekends spent recovering from injury at home are not as much fun as Saturdays on the fairways. Dedicate yourself to getting fit and preventing injury.

D A V I D   H E R M A N

Introduction

THE PROFESSIONAL GOLFER AND the working golfer both, inevitably, are plagued by golf's greatest occupational hazard: *injury.* While not perceived as a strenuous activity or a physically grueling sport, golf certainly has its physical risks for its growing millions of participants. Golfers come in all sizes, ages, shapes, levels of physical ability, and fitness levels—and all of these characteristics are factors in the frequency and type of injury. While golf is not a hazardous sport, golfers do sustain injuries and feel pain (suffering is another topic).

Why? Because the golf swing and its mechanics are demanding and vigorous. And, often, the most diligent (or obsessed) of us practice incorrectly, or in spurts, or for too long. Ernie and I agree that most injuries in golf can be either prevented entirely or, at least, reduced by a careful combination of:

- proper swing mechanics
- intelligent practice routines
- gaining and maintaining a fit, healthy body

Fitness and all its components—strength, flexibility, cardiovascular conditioning—remain a key to injury prevention. But it's also very important that we consider our history of injuries—our old war wounds—when designing an exercise program. For example, Ernie has an injury to his right shoulder that occurred while he was playing cricket. Whenever he throws a football, hits a tennis serve, or does certain lifting exercises above his shoulder, there's a chance he'll aggravate his old injury. So we're very careful to either stay away from these exercises entirely or use very light weights when we do them.

But injuries are a part of life and a part of the game of golf. They can occur randomly while lifting your golf bag out of the car, sleeping in the wrong position, swinging vigorously without the proper warm-up, or even hitting a root or a rock during a swing.

Injuries can often be a result of bad technique: gripping the club too hard; planting your feet improperly; a hitch or jerk in your swing; and, quite often, overcompensating for another injury or pain. Excessive, repetitive practice coupled with bad technique (swing mechanics) can also send you home hurting.

What to Do If You Feel Pain

REST

Usually, the first strategy if you feel pain or discomfort is to rest. If you try to push through an injury, you'll probably only make it worse. As we've said before, it's a lot easier to prevent an injury than it is to heal one. Of course, if pain persists, rest might not be enough.

ICE

Applying ice is a great way to reduce swelling, decrease pain, and promote healing. You should ice an injured area as quickly as possible. Be careful not to ice longer than twenty minutes, and never ice an injured area before hitting balls or engaging in other strenuous activity. Before working out, your muscles, joints, and tendons need to be warmed up, not cooled down. If you feel you need to ice to play, you probably shouldn't be playing.

HEAT

Heat is used to increase circulation to an injured area. By using heat for ten to fifteen minutes, you can increase blood flow and loosen up the tight muscles, tendons, and joints. By warming up an area, you're less likely to aggravate an old injury or cause a new one. Heat can be applied by using a heating pad, standing under a hot shower, or soaking the injured area in a warm bath or whirlpool. You don't want to apply heat just after an injury has happened. This can delay healing by causing inflammation in the area. Wait twenty-four to forty-eight hours before using heat. However, if you absolutely *must* play with an injury, generally you want to heat up the injured area before hitting balls.

OTHER ALTERNATIVES

You may want to consider taking a pain reliever, such as ibuprofen, when you're injured. There are a variety of different products that help to decrease inflammation and promote healing. Of course, these products aren't an end in themselves. They should be used in addition to other recovery and healing techniques.

A gentle massage can also help to promote healing and increase circulation. But you must be careful not to get massage treatment too soon after the injury occurs. As with heat, massage can cause more swelling and delay the healing process.

Once your injury is better, you're going to want to ease back into your workout routine. Be very careful not to overdo it at the gym at this time. Start slow and keep the weight light. If your injury continues to bother you, please see your doctor. Your doctor can help you determine exactly what is wrong. If your injury is serious enough, you may need professional help to overcome it.

The Common Injuries

Studies have shown us that the most commonly injured body part for the golfer is the lower back, followed by the shoulder, the hand/wrist, the elbows, and the knees. Add the occasional neck and foot injury and you begin to realize how intensely you utilize your body while playing golf.

Back

Just ask Ernie about back trouble. Ernie had his first serious back problem in June 1998 while he was at the top of his game and ranked among the top three golfers in the world. What happened? He felt a twinge on the plane traveling from Dallas to London. A few weeks later, he arrived at the Buick Open in Harrison, New York, to defend his consecutive titles and didn't last long on the practice range. His back was sore and irritated him every time he swung. The rest of the season was one aggravation after another. Nagging pains and the mental awareness of discomfort all altered his swing and his game. Ernie began to struggle.

Research indicates that 70 percent of us experience back pain during our lives, whether it is minor muscle strain or a slipped disk. And no wonder. The back is a delicate and complicated structure. It is made up of twenty-four individual vertebrae separated by flexible disks, layers of muscle, ligaments, tendons, and countless joints. The spinal cord controls nerves, which carry signals to the brain and the rest of the body. When pain erupts in the back, the rest of your body is notified rapidly!

Office life can also put stress on your back. Tense telephone conversations with the receiver buried in your neck and regularly sitting slouched in your chair can add to back tightness, soreness, or even chronic pain.

Adapting and correcting can save wear and tear on the joints and muscles.

Ernie and I recommend five simple prevention techniques:

• Strengthen your core muscle groups to protect your lower back.
• Make sure you have proper posture while standing, sitting, and during physical activity.
• Be physically fit.
• Maintain a reasonable weight.
• Always protect your back when lifting heavy objects.

Back exercises—which we will detail for you in this chapter—should focus on good technique, light weight, and targeted stretching. Further, you must concentrate on technique in your golf game. Good mechanics can eliminate herky-jerky movements and improve both your practice sessions and your rounds of golf. Consider **posture** an important component of your pain-free goal. Make sure you are standing, sitting, and walking correctly. Check your setup!

Also, be aware of your everyday activities to make sure you are protecting your back. I mentioned bending over to lift your golf bag out of the trunk. Do it carefully and intelligently.

Be aware of your back when you travel. Leave your plane or train seat and stretch, or if you're driving, pull over at a rest stop if you feel like you are tightening up. Think about your sleep habits and how you sit at your desk for hours each day. Is your spine in the proper position? If you're having back problems, these things could be causing them. If you have chronic pain, we suggest consulting a professional who can make an accurate diagnosis. It could be an orthopedist, a physical therapist, or even a chiropractor—whatever you're comfortable with.

Think also of protecting your spine throughout the course of your normal week. Are you careful when shoveling snow or digging in the garden? Are you cautious when lifting the weights off the rack or carrying heavy suitcases? When you exercise, are you strengthening your back muscles effectively and properly?

When you're healing from a back injury, your fitness program should focus on light aerobic exercises that do not place excess stress on the back. If you immediately jump back into your old workout routine at full intensity, you risk tweaking your old injury. You should also pay special attention to cautiously working the muscles in your back and abdomen—they need to be strengthened and stretched. Try incorporating some of these lower back exercises into your routine.

Lower Back Exercises and Stretches

(Strengthening the abdominals is very important for protecting the lower back. See also Reverse Ab Tilt with Ball on page 82 and Upper Ab Curl with Ball on page 84.)

Opposite Arm and Leg Raise

Kneel on all fours, relaxed, with a natural arch in your lower back. Raise your right arm and left leg simultaneously to a position parallel to the floor or to a point where your back is challenged by holding the position (Figure 1). Hold the position and maintain the tension for 3 seconds, then slowly lower your arm and leg to the starting position. Repeat the process with the opposite arm and leg (Figure 2).

FIGURE 1

NOTES

- Keep your head and neck in a neutral position.
- Begin with 1 set and advance to 2; do 10 to 15 repetitions on each side.

Golf-fit benefit: This is an excellent trunk stabilization exercise that strengthens the muscles that protect the lower back.

FIGURE 2   *Notice how the arm and leg are fully extended and pointed.*

Cat Stretch

Targeted Muscle Group

This exercise stretches the erector spinae (lower back muscles).

Technique

Kneel on all fours with your lower back in a relaxed (tucked down) position (Figure 1). Keeping your head lowered, round the back, extending it upward toward the ceiling (Figure 2). While maintaining the arch in the back, tilt backward, sitting on the heels, and exhale (Figure 3). Return to the starting position. Repeat 5 to 10 times.

FIGURE 1

FIGURE 2

FIGURE 3

Lower Back Hyperextension

A good stretch to do along with this exercise is Lower Back Rotational Stretch on page 108.

Targeted Muscle Group

This is an excellent exercise to strengthen the erector spinae (lower back muscles).

Technique

Lie flat on the floor on your stomach with your arms placed next to the body. Contract the lower back muscle (above your waist) and raise your head, chest, and shoulders off the floor, slightly arching your back. Hold the tension for 3 seconds and slowly lower the trunk to the starting position. Do 1 or 2 sets of 10 to 30 repetitions, depending on your level of fitness.

Shoulder

The most common shoulder injury for a right-handed golfer is a rotator cuff strain on the left side. The rotator cuff is the part of your shoulder responsible for allowing the rotation of your arm. When the rotator cuff becomes strained, one or more of the four rotator cuff tendons in your shoulder becomes inflamed. This is caused by repetitive swinging of the clubs, which eventually wears down the tendons. Symptoms include pain and the limited movement of the shoulder. The golfer's hands go above the shoulder on both the backswing and the follow-through, so this area must be protected against injury. Building up the muscles that surround the rotator cuff—as we're about to show you how—is the best way to prevent this injury from occurring. Please note that when using light weights, the Dumbbell Lateral Raise (page 78) and Rear Deltoid Fly (page 79) are also excellent exercises for strengthening the rotator cuff.

Shoulder Exercises and Stretches

Towel Stretch

Targeted Muscle Group

This exercise is used to stretch the shoulder internally.

Technique

Grasp a towel at both ends and hold it behind your back. Raise your right arm overhead and reach toward the ceiling. Your left lower arm (which is still behind your back) will rise up along the spine. Hold, then switch arm positions and repeat. Hold each stretch for 10 to 20 seconds. Repeat 1 to 2 times.

External Shoulder Rotation

Targeted Muscle Group

This exercise strengthens the muscles that protect the rotator cuff.

FIGURE 1

Technique

Stand with your arms hanging at your sides. Bend your right elbow until your right arm is in a 90-degree position. Support your right elbow (and arm) on your left arm and hand (Figure 1). Holding the cable with your right hand, turn your hand out to the right, externally rotating the shoulder (Figure 2). Switch arms and repeat. Do 1 or 2 sets of 20 repetitions. Make sure to use light resistance.

FIGURE 2

Internal Shoulder Rotation

Targeted Muscle Group

This exercise strengthens the muscles that protect the rotator cuff.

FIGURE 1

Technique

Stand with your left elbow bent at 90 degrees away from the body and resting on your right hand. Press your left arm firmly against the supporting right hand (Figure 1). Holding the cable in the left hand, turn the arm to the right and across, internally rotating the shoulder (Figure 2). Slowly return to the starting position. Switch arms and repeat. Do 1 or 2 sets of 15 to 20 repetitions.

FIGURE 2

Scaption

Targeted Muscle Group

This exercise strengthens the supraspinatus, which helps protect the rotator cuff.

Technique

With your right arm about 30 degrees to the side (Figure 1), raise a light dumbbell to your shoulder's height, keeping your thumb pointed up (Figure 2). Hold for 2 seconds, then slowly lower to the starting position. Do 1 or 2 sets of 15 to 25 repetitions, or until you fatigue.

FIGURE 1

FIGURE 2

Corner Stretch

Targeted Muscle Groups

This exercise stretches the muscles of the chest and shoulder.

Technique

Bend your elbows to 90 degrees and stand facing the corner of a room. Place an elbow and forearm on each wall, with your body facing the corner. Lean forward toward the corner, allowing your body to relax. Be creative with the elbow and hand positions to feel different stretches. Perform this stretch for between 10 and 20 seconds. Repeat 2 times.

Elbow, Forearm, and Wrist

Elbow pain can often be caused by the sudden impact of the club hitting the ground. It can also be caused by poor swing mechanics. Both these things can damage the elbow tendons. "Golfer's elbow" is usually pain on the outside of the left elbow (for the right-handed golfer). "Tennis elbow" pain is pain on the inside of the elbow. Both are the result of inflammation that usually occurs where the tendon attaches to the bone.

In any event, when an elbow injury occurs, you need to rest and not aggravate it. Next, you need to examine your swing mechanics and make sure your technique is correct. That will help solve the problem and the pain.

Finally, you must strengthen the wrist and forearm muscles with exercise. You will also want to tone and strengthen the muscles of the upper arm and shoulder.

Wrist and Forearm Exercises

(Note: With all of these exercises, if you feel discomfort in your elbow, reduce the amount of weight. If you feel pain, stop immediately. You may need to have your elbow evaluated by a professional.)

Wrist Curl

Targeted Muscle Groups

This exercise strengthens the muscles of the wrist and the forearm.

Technique

Holding a dumbbell, place the back of your right forearm on a bench or table, palm facing up. The wrist and hand should be over the edge. Lift the weight by flexing the wrist, then lower it to the starting position (Figure 1). Change hands and repeat. Do 1 or 2 sets of 15 to 20 repetitions.

NOTE

- For a variation (Reverse Wrist Curl), you can turn your forearm over and flex your wrist up and back (Figure 2).

FIGURE 1

FIGURE 2

FIGURE 1

Dumbbell Forearm Curl

Targeted Muscle Groups

This exercise strengthens the muscles of the wrist and forearm.

Technique

Standing up, with a light weight in your right hand, place your left arm under your right elbow for support (Figure 1). To raise the weight, contract the muscles in your forearm (Figure 2). Slowly return the weight to the starting position. Switch arms and repeat. The weight should be held at a slight outward angle. Do 1 or 2 sets of 15 to 20 repetitions. Use a lighter weight than you used for the Wrist Curl.

FIGURE 2

Forearm Supination and Pronation

Targeted Muscle Groups

This exercise strengthens the muscles that rotate the wrist and the forearm.

Technique

Stand holding a club with your right arm extended (Figure 1). Hold the club at grip with the right hand, the club head facing the ceiling, and slowly rotate the club to the left until it is parallel to the ground and your fingers are facing down (Figure 2). Then slowly rotate the club in the opposite direction until it is once again parallel to the ground. Add a second club if more tension is desired. Change hands and repeat the exercise. Do 1 or 2 sets of 15 to 20 repetitions.

FIGURE 1

FIGURE 2

Wrist Flexion Stretch

Targeted Muscle Groups

This exercise stretches the muscles of the wrists and forearms.

Technique

Stand straight, feet shoulder width apart, knees slightly bent. With your right arm extended out in front of your body, palm facing down and wrist cocked back to a 90-degree angle, reach with your left hand and pull back the fingers of the right until a deep stretch is felt in the forearm. Repeat, switching arms. Do this stretch 1 or 2 times, each for 15 seconds.

Wrist and Forearm Stretch

Targeted Muscle Groups

This exercise stretches the muscles of the wrists and forearms.

Technique

Stand straight, feet shoulder width apart, knees slightly bent. With the right arm extended out in front of the body, palm facing down and wrist cocked down at a 90-degree angle, reach with the left hand and slowly pull back the right hand until a deep stretch is felt in the top of the forearm. Repeat, switching arms. Do this stretch 1 or 2 times, each for 15 seconds.

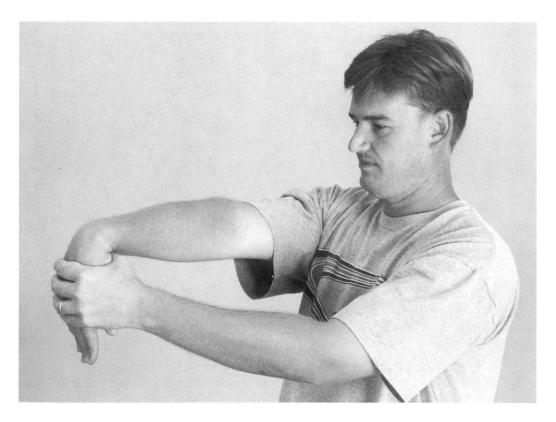

CHAPTER EIGHT

Workout Programs

ON THE FOLLOWING PAGES we will set forth a series of exercise programs for you to consider using in your workout regimen. As we said in chapter 5, the general exercises target the major muscle groups of the body and are best used when you are beginning a new workout program or phasing back into your old one. Once you have gradually and comfortably worked yourself into good shape, you can move over to the golf-specific exercise programs. But it's a good idea to concentrate on building a solid foundation with these general exercises.

If you are not familiar with gym equipment or lifting techniques, I would highly recommend using a personal trainer for a period of time until you feel you are ready to tackle them on your own.

Here are some key thoughts to focus on the first day back at the gym:

- Work on the larger muscle groups, such as the chest, shoulders, back, legs, and abdominals.

- Err on the side of caution—don't make yourself too sore.

- One to two sets of strength and endurance exercises (preceded by warm-up) should be plenty the first day.

Also, it is important to remember, the better your technique, the faster your results will come. But don't expect them on the first day. Or even the first week. After three workouts or so you should notice your strength and endurance coming back. And the good news is that muscles have a memory. The younger you are, the shorter the time it takes to get back to the same level. If you slack off for six months, you can come back within a month if you are in your twenties, slightly over a month in your thirties and early forties, and nearly two months if you are over fifty. The reason for this is that your body's growth hormone naturally diminishes as you get older, so recovery takes a little longer.

Whether you are a first-time weight lifter or an experienced gym rat, remember to start with light weights and keep your repetitions high. Move slowly through the up and down phases of the exercises. Try to fatigue in the fifteen- to twenty-repetition range. If you have started with too much weight and get only to ten repetitions, you will increase your chances for deep muscular soreness. Be sure that you can *easily* do one set of fifteen to twenty repetitions, feeling the burn only at the end of the repetitions. Be careful not to overdo it. There's a very thin line between muscle fibers that are breaking down due to strength training (a good thing) and a muscle strain that can lead to serious soreness or even injury. By keeping the weight light, you stay on the right side of this fine line.

It's also a good idea to vary the angle at which you're working your muscles by using a variety of equipment and exercises for each body part. For example, one time in the gym you might want to use free weights, and the next time you might want to do the machine or cable equivalent of the same exercise. This makes your workouts more challenging and entertaining and will lead to better muscular balance and development.

Here are a few suggested routines:

GENERAL EXERCISE PROGRAM, LEVEL I

Day #1
Monday or Tuesday

CARDIO

10 minutes of warm-up (steady-state), followed by 10 to 15 minutes of low-to-moderate-intensity intervals, followed by a 3-minute cooldown

STRENGTH TRAINING (1 TO 2 SETS EACH)

Upper Body

Dumbbell Chest Press (page 50)
Dumbbell Shoulder Press (page 52)
Seated Lat Row (page 54)
Triceps Press-Down (page 57)
Dumbbell Biceps Curl (page 58)

Lower Body

Leg Press (page 60)
Leg Extension (page 62)
Leg Curl (page 64)
Standing Calf Raise (page 66)

Core

Upper Ab Curl (page 70)
Hyperextension (page 72)

FLEXIBILITY TRAINING

Chest Stretch (page 100)
Lat Stretch (page 101)
Hamstring Stretch (page 103)
Quad Stretch (page 104)

Day #2
Wednesday or Thursday

CARDIO

10 minutes of warm-up, followed by 10 to 25 minutes of low-to-moderate-intensity intervals, followed by a 3-minute cooldown

Core (2 to 3 sets each)

Lower Ab Tilt with Bench (page 68)
Upper Ab Curl (page 70)
Hip Abduction (page 94)
Hip Adduction (page 92)
Opposite Arm and Leg Raise (page 118)
Hyperextension (page 72)

FLEXIBILITY TRAINING

Hamstring Stretch (page 103)
Glute Stretch (page 105)
Hip Adductor Stretch (page 107)
Hip Flexor Stretch (page 106)
Cat Stretch (page 120)
Lower Back Rotational Stretch (page 108)
Upper Back Rotational Stretch (page 109)

Day #3
Friday or Saturday

CARDIO

10 minutes of warm-up, followed by 10 to 25 minutes of low-to-moderate-intensity intervals, followed by a 3-minute cooldown

STRENGTH TRAINING (1 TO 2 SETS EACH)

Upper Body

Dumbbell Chest Press (page 50)
Dumbbell Shoulder Press (page 52)
Lat Pull-Down (page 56)
Triceps Press-Down (page 57)
Dumbbell Biceps Curl (page 58)

Lower Body

Leg Press (page 60)
Leg Extension (page 62)
Leg Curl (page 64)
Standing Calf Raise (page 66)

Core

Upper Ab Curl (page 70)
Hyperextension (page 72)

FLEXIBILITY TRAINING

Chest Stretch (page 100)
Bent-Over Shoulder Stretch (page 102)
Hamstring Stretch (page 103)
Quad Stretch (page 104)

Note: For body fat loss, add an additional 10 minutes of low-intensity cardio before flexibility training. Also, each strength training exercise should be preceded by a warm-up set.

GENERAL EXERCISE PROGRAM, LEVEL II

Day #1	Day #2
Monday and Thursday	Tuesday and Friday

Day #1 — Monday and Thursday

CARDIO

10 minutes of steady-state, followed by 15 to 20 minutes of moderate-to-higher-intensity intervals, followed by a 3-minute cooldown

STRENGTH TRAINING (2 TO 3 SETS EACH)

Upper Body and Core

Dumbbell Chest Press (page 50)
Dumbbell Shoulder Press (page 52)
Dumbbell Lateral Raise (page 78)
Rear Deltoid Fly (page 79)
Seated Lat Row (page 54) or Lat Pull-Down (page 56)

For the exercises below, 1 to 2 sets are enough.

Triceps Press-Down (page 57)
Dumbbell Biceps Curl (page 58)
Forearm Curl (page 81)
Wrist Curl (page 130)
Lower Ab Tilt with Bench (page 68)
Upper Ab Curl (page 70)
Hyperextension (page 72)

FLEXIBILITY TRAINING

Chest Stretch (page 100)
Hanging Lat Stretch (page 110)
Lat Stretch (page 101)
Bent-Over Shoulder Stretch (page 102)

Day #2 — Tuesday and Friday

CARDIO

10 minutes of steady-state, followed by 15 to 20 minutes of moderate-to-higher-intensity intervals, followed by a 3-minute cooldown

STRENGTH TRAINING (2 TO 3 SETS EACH)

Lower Body and Core

Leg Press (page 60)
Leg Extension (page 62)
Leg Curl (page 64)

For the exercises below, 1 to 2 sets are enough.

Hip Adduction (page 92)
Hip Abduction (page 94)
Standing Calf Raise (page 66)
Lower Ab Tilt with Bench (page 68)
Upper Ab Curl (page 70)
Diagonal Trunk Rotation with Band (page 86)
Hyperextension (page 72)

FLEXIBILITY TRAINING

Hamstring Stretch (page 103)
Quad Stretch (page 104)
Glute Stretch (page 105)
Hip Adductor Stretch (page 107)

Note: For body fat loss, add an additional 10 minutes of low-intensity cardio before flexibility training. Also, each strength training exercise should be preceded by a warm-up set.

GOLF-SPECIFIC PROGRAM, LEVEL I

Day #1

Monday or Tuesday

CARDIO

Follow the general program, Day #1.

STRENGTH TRAINING (2 TO 3 SETS)

Upper Body

Chest Fly (page 74)
Seated Lat Row (page 54)
Dumbbell Lateral Raise
  (page 78)
Rear Deltoid Fly (page 79)
Triceps Press-Down
  (page 57)

1 to 2 sets are enough from here down.

Forearm Curl (page 81)
Wrist Curl (page 130)

Core

Reverse Ab Tilt with Ball
  (page 82)
Upper Ab Curl with Ball
  (page 84)
Diagonal Trunk Rotation
  with Band (page 86)
Opposite Arm and Leg
  Raise (page 118)
Lower Back Hyperextension
  on Ball (page 88)

Day #2

Wednesday or Thursday

CARDIO

Follow the general program, Day #1.

STRENGTH TRAINING (2 TO 3 SETS)

Lower Body

Leg Press (page 60) or
  Exerball Wall Squat
  (page 90)
Leg Extension (page 62)
Leg Curl (page 64)
Hip Adduction (page 92)
Hip Abduction (page 94)

Core

Reverse Ab Tilt with Ball
  (page 82)
Upper Ab Curl with Ball
  (page 84)
Lower Back Hyperextension
  on Ball (page 88)

Day #3

Friday or Saturday

CARDIO

Follow the general program, Day #1.

STRENGTH TRAINING (2 TO 3 SETS)

Upper Body

Chest Fly (page 74)
Dumbbell Lateral Raise
  (page 78)
Seated Lat Row (page 54)
Rear Deltoid Fly (page 79)
Internal Shoulder Rotation
  (page 126)
External Shoulder Rotation
  (page 124)

Lower Body

Leg Press (page 60)

1 to 2 sets are enough from here down.

Hip Adduction (page 92)
Hip Abduction (page 94)

Core

Reverse Ab Tilt with Ball
  (page 82)
Upper Ab Curl with Ball
  (page 84)
Diagonal Trunk Rotation
  with Band (page 86)
Opposite Arm and Leg
  Raise (page 118)
Lower Back Hyperextension
  (page 122)

GOLF-SPECIFIC PROGRAM, LEVEL I *(continued)*

Day #1	Day #2	Day #3
FLEXIBILITY TRAINING	**FLEXIBILITY TRAINING**	**FLEXIBILITY TRAINING**
Chest Stretch (page 100)	Hamstring Stretch (page 103)	Target your tight areas.
Lat Stretch (page 101)	Quad Stretch (page 104)	
Cat Stretch (page 120)	Glute Stretch (page 105)	
Lower Back Rotational Stretch (page 108)	Hip Adductor Stretch (page 107)	
	Cat Stretch (page 120)	
	Upper Back Rotational Stretch (page 109)	

GOLF-SPECIFIC PROGRAM, LEVEL II

Note: This is a higher-level workout to try when you are really looking for a good stretch.

CARDIO

10 minutes of steady-state, followed by 10 to 15 minutes of moderate-to-high-intensity intervals

STRENGTH TRAINING/ FLEXIBILITY TRAINING

Each strength training set is immediately followed by a stretching exercise. Hold each stretch for 20 seconds. For example, do a warm-up set of the Chest Fly, then do your first set of the Chest Fly. Immediately after, do the Chest Stretch for your right side. Do your second set of flies, then do the Chest Stretch for your left side.

Chest Fly (page 74)/Chest Stretch (page 100)
Seated Lat Row (page 54)/ Lat Stretch (page 101)
Rear Deltoid Fly (page 79)/Bent-Over Shoulder Stretch (page 102)
Leg Extension (page 62)/ Quad Stretch (page 104)
Leg Curl (page 64)/ Hamstring Stretch (page 103)
Lower Back Hyperextension on Ball (page 88)/Cat Stretch (page 120)
Opposite Arm and Leg Raise (page 118)/Lower Back Rotational Stretch (page 108) *(optional)*
Hip Adduction (page 92)/ Hip Adductor Stretch (page 107)
Hip Abduction (page 94)/ Hip Flexor Stretch (page 106)

Core

Lower Ab Tilt with Bench (page 68)
Upper Ab Curl (page 70)
Diagonal Trunk Rotation with Band (page 86)

CHAPTER NINE

Nutrition

A Few Helpful Guidelines

I think I'm an expert on how not to eat. I love food and have no inhibitions about occasionally chowing down. But moderation and careful choices can create a healthy diet and body. Eat smart, exercise properly, and your stamina and concentration on the golf course and in the office will be improved.

ERNIE ELS

Introduction

THERE ARE MANY COMPLICATED THEORIES about sports nutrition. But we just want to get across a few simple points. The most important one is that no matter how much time you spend working out, unless you feed your body properly, you're not going to perform at your best. In the end, it's up to you. We're not asking you to change your eating habits. We would merely like to pass on some commonsense tips regarding eating, drinking, supplements, and healthy snacks.

Here are a few ideas to help you out in the gym and on the course:

- Always eat breakfast—even if it's just a protein bar as you're walking out the door.
- Don't arrive at the course too hungry or too full.
- Eat small, healthy snacks (sports drinks, nutrition bars) during your four-hour round to stabilize your blood sugar.
- Drink lots of water (8 glasses a day), especially when playing.
- Avoid foods with high sugar content while in the gym or on the course. Candy bars or soda will give you a kick, but will result in low blood sugar levels and will leave you fatigued and unfocused.
- Alcohol causes dehydration and fatigue, so avoid it while playing seriously. Of course, if you're just hitting a few balls with your friends . . .

Nutritional Program

Together, good nutrition and fluid replacement are essential to your performance, especially when it comes to athletics. If you really want to be at your best day in and day out, you must follow a balanced nutritional program.

Every program will differ according to your body's specific needs, but they all include a balance of carbohydrates, proteins, and fat. Learn to read nutritional levels to help you get a sense of what you're putting in your body.

At the top levels, many athletes have precise eating routines that involve eating up to five or six times throughout the course of the day. These meals include your basic breakfast, lunch, and dinner and two or three snacks in between and before you go to bed. Your main meal should be early in the day, and your last meal should be early in the evening (be careful to avoid eating complex carbohydrates, such as bread, potatoes, and pasta, late at night). When you eat this way, you will digest your food more quickly and efficiently, and your metabolism will speed up as well. Another benefit is that stabilizing your blood sugar levels will help balance your energy levels and keep you focused and on track. Your body will also have a constant supply of protein throughout the day, and protein helps muscles repair themselves.

Karen Palacios, an LPGA instructor at the Jim McLean Golf School at the Doral Resort and Spa, says that one of the main performance-related problems she constantly observes is eating, and fueling, the body properly:

When people come to the golf school we begin our program at 8:00 A.M. During the morning session they have nothing to eat, and by noon they are starving. At lunch they overeat by consuming high-fat foods and lots of sugar (colas, juices, and caffeine). They go out to play in the afternoon and they are sluggish. Their performance is clearly not as good as it was in the morning. I tell them to bring small snacks to the course and to eat a lighter midday meal. And by all means, stay away from burgers, colas, and dessert at lunch!

And don't forget the water. Next to the air you breathe, water is the key requirement for energy and survival. The common rule of thumb is to drink eight glasses of water a day. Keep in mind that the colder the water, the faster it gets into your system. And make sure to drink water before, during, and after exercise—even in cooler weather.

Supplements, Sports Drinks, Protein Bars

A number of products are sold at health food stores, drugstores, nutrition stores, and specialty food shops to help increase energy levels, to promote fat loss, and to add lean muscle mass. These include a vast line of herbal products, multivitamins, and other dietary supplements. Some work, some might work, and many have not been appropriately tested and approved by the federal Food and Drug Administration. So be cautious and seek advice from your nutritionist or doctor.

Protein bars are available everywhere. They are a balanced source of proteins, carbohydrates, and fats. Try a variety and choose the healthy ones you like. They are especially useful when you're traveling, playing, or working out for a long period of time.

Protein shakes are a good supplement if you need to get out the door quickly. They are also a great post-workout drink. They provide a balanced, fast way to replenish depleted nutrients and promote recovery.

Sports drinks provide electrolytes, sodium replacement, and simple carbohydrates that quickly get into your system. They can help you boost and maintain your energy levels over a longer period of time.

Some herbal products promote fat loss and increase energy levels. These can help push you through your workout. Take a look and consult an expert if you have questions about the benefits (or potential side effects) of these products.

Creatine is a controversial supplement used to promote lean muscle mass and strength gains, and many athletes use it, even golfers (during the off-season). While golfers obviously aren't looking to bulk up, they may still be able to benefit from the decreased recovery time between workouts that creatine-enhanced strength gains provide. Before taking creatine, consult a nutrionist.

In Conclusion

Make sure to eat well around your workouts. Unless you're looking to maximize fat burning, eat a good meal one and a half to two hours before your workout. After your workout, you want to eat as soon as possible, even if it's just an energy or protein bar. This helps replenish depleted carbohydrate (glycogen) stores and promotes faster recovery. Always keep in mind that there's no better way to improve than to eat and train like a world-class athlete.

Index

About the Authors

ERNIE ELS is a two-time winner of the U.S. Open and winner of more than twenty other tournaments in ten years of professional golf. He lives in Johannesburg, South Africa, and Orlando, Florida.

DAVID HERMAN is a sports conditioning consultant for several world-class athletes. He lives in Orlando, Florida. His Web site is GolfandBody.com.